C000138840

"Combining their interdisciplinary heritage [...]
psychology, Deans, Frydenberg and Lian[...]
scholarly publication that will be welcom[...]
young children and their families. Given the complex challenges impacting
family life in contemporary society, this text offers much needed guidance in
strengthening the social and emotional well-being of young children.
Research-rich insights provoke thinking and provide a sound platform for
considering suggestions that are practical and relevant to today's families. The
warmth of intergenerational nurturing and reciprocal nature of these relationships are beautifully captured in this text. Recommended as an essential text
for initial teacher education as well as continuing professional development of
experienced teachers, social workers and psychologists."

Professor Manjula Waniganayake, Professor of Early Childhood
Education, Macquarie University, Australia

"*Promoting Well-Being in the Pre-School Years* opens the doors for positive
education and positive psychology practices in early childhood education,
and provides an innovative theory and research-driven resource to build
well-being in young children through social and emotional learning.
A child's ability to successfully cope with day-to-day difficulties and challenges is a fundamental proficiency that should be prioritised alongside
STEM and literacy in the classroom. Like academic skills, social and emotional competencies can be taught, and the earlier the better. This book
provides essential know-how for educators and parents who want to support the development of healthy flourishing children."

Dr Kelly-Ann Allen, Senior Lecturer, Educational Psychology and
Inclusive Education, Faculty of Education, Monash University

Promoting Well-Being in the Pre-School Years

Promoting Well-Being in the Pre-School Years provides evidence-based research and real-life strategies that support social and emotional development and well-being for children aged 3–5 years. It places emphasis on nurturing social emotional competence through purposeful scaffolding activities and how these can be used by children and families to create a harmonious platform for building resilience and positive relationships with family and the community.

Drawing on principles from Positive Psychology and Positive Education, it is illustrated throughout with examples of sustainable practice in diverse, global settings. Key topics explored include:

* Contemporary well-being concepts, including 'grit', 'growth mindset' and 'gratitude', as well as 'classic' constructs such as coping and self-efficacy
* The attitudes and skills that need to be developed to ensure that young children flourish
* Cognitive and sociocultural perspectives complemented by neuroscience and epigenetics
* Social Emotional Learning (SEL) in the early years curriculum
* Using visual tools – the Early Years Coping Cards
* How we measure young children's coping
* The relationship between coping, stress and mental health
* Recognition of the importance of parents' own coping skills
* How partnerships with communities can improve children's SEL.

Promoting Well-Being in the Pre-School Years shows how we can support young children to develop an understanding of what it means to be happy and to flourish as a socially responsible member of the family and wider community. It is essential reading for teachers, parents and professionals who work with young children, as well as academics in child development.

Erica Frydenberg is Associate Professor in psychology in the Melbourne Graduate School of Education, University of Melbourne, Australia.

Janice Deans is Associate Director, Early Childhood Education, University of Melbourne, Australia.

Rachel Liang is Honorary Research Fellow, Melbourne Graduate School of Education, University of Melbourne, Australia.

Promoting Well-Being in the Pre-School Years

Research, Applications and Strategies

Erica Frydenberg, Janice Deans and Rachel Liang

Routledge
Taylor & Francis Group

LONDON AND NEW YORK

First published 2020
by Routledge
2 Park Square, Milton Park, Abingdon, Oxon, OX14 4RN

and by Routledge
52 Vanderbilt Avenue, New York, NY 10017

Routledge is an imprint of the Taylor & Francis Group, an informa business

© 2020 Erica Frydenberg, Janice Deans and Rachel Liang

The right of Erica Frydenberg, Janice Deans and Rachel Liang to
be identified as authors of this work has been asserted by them
in accordance with sections 77 and 78 of the Copyright, Designs
and Patents Act 1988.

All rights reserved. No part of this book may be reprinted or
reproduced or utilised in any form or by any electronic,
mechanical, or other means, now known or hereafter invented,
including photocopying and recording, or in any information
storage or retrieval system, without permission in writing from
the publishers.

Trademark notice: Product or corporate names may be
trademarks or registered trademarks, and are used only for
identification and explanation without intent to infringe.

British Library Cataloguing-in-Publication Data
A catalogue record for this book is available from the British Library

Library of Congress Cataloging-in-Publication Data
A catalog record for this title has been requested

ISBN: 978-0-367-02862-6 (hbk)
ISBN: 978-0-367-02863-3 (pbk)
ISBN: 978-0-429-01918-0 (ebk)

Typeset in Garamond
by Swales & Willis, Exeter, Devon, UK

MIX
Paper from
responsible sources
FSC   FSC™ C013985

Printed in the United Kingdom
by Henry Ling Limited

Contents

Figures

Tables

Foreword

It does not seem that long ago when the main purpose of pre-school (and similar early childhood services) was to look after young children while their parents were at work. Then, as we gained greater understanding of the educational opportunities afforded by pre-school, its purpose evolved to one also focused on teaching the personal and basic academic skills needed for children's first year at school. In the past decade, its purpose has evolved again. In addition to preparing young children for school, pre-schools now also seek to develop the social and emotional skills that are needed for life.

Thus, much more is expected of pre-schools today – and for good reason: there is a substantial evidence base demonstrating that these are critical years in which to foster and sustain social and emotional well-being Indeed, this evidence emphasizes that a healthy start to life has long and positive reach into the school years – and beyond. Accordingly, there is a strong need for substantial and comprehensive resources that progress current understanding and practice in this space. The present volume does just this. It draws on high quality and up-to-date research and practitioner insights to develop a most timely and necessary resource for promoting young children's well-being

Over the past decade there have been major efforts aimed at clarifying salient well-being concepts and constructs important to target in the early years. These include 'grit', 'flourishing', 'growth mindsets', and 'gratitude'. This volume dedicates significant attention to research and practice relevant to these (and more) constructs and so represents a highly contemporary account of well-being in the pre-school years. Moreover, not only does the volume attend to these 'new-generation' constructs, it complements these with continued and important attention to 'classic' constructs (such as self-efficacy, coping, etc.). In so doing, it ensures a well-rounded approach to well-being that brings together the best of what we have long known and what latest research and practice are adding to this knowledge. Indeed, the team of Frydenberg (coping), Deans (early childhood), and Liang (positive psychology in professional practice) ensure expert coverage of the constructs that are critical for young children's development.

The comprehensive nature of this volume is further underscored by the range of theory on which it draws and the range of applications and contexts implicated in childhood well-being With regard to theory, the well-established cognitive and sociocultural perspectives are explained, complemented by more recent contributions around neuroscience and epigenetics. In terms of context, the volume has global dimensions, with well-being practices in early childhood being considered from numerous national perspectives — and at the more local level, it closely considers applications in the home and in educational environments.

Another major feature of this volume is its focus on the means by which well-being is to be promoted in early childhood. There is ongoing debate on whether social and emotional well-being should be taught explicitly through targeted and dedicated programs, or whether it should be embedded in the ordinary course of curriculum and pedagogy. The practical nature of this volume is highlighted in its attention to both explicit and embedded approaches to promoting well-being It also provides guidance on how parents can promote their children's well-being including recognition of the importance of parents' own coping skills and the cross-generational dimensions of this.

Taken together, this book provides educators, parents, and other professionals with a substantial understanding of what is involved in teaching social and emotional skills to young children. It supports this understanding with take-home messages at the end of each chapter and with tools and practical examples on how to promote well-being in diverse settings. It is an outstanding resource supporting social and emotional well-being at a time in life when children are highly receptive to quality intervention and practice.

Andrew J. Martin

Scientia Professor and Professor of Educational Psychology

University of New South Wales, Australia

Preface

Childhood well-being sets the foundation for later health, social, emotional and educational outcomes. Much attention of early years learning is focused on the importance of early social emotional skill development as a precursor for later educational success and other key successful life outcomes. This book is an outcome of a decade of evidence-based research and real-life applications and practice of strategies that support social and emotional development and well-being for children aged 3–5 years. Drawing on the principles from Positive Education and the literature surrounding coping and resilience, the vast body of research and practice in our work since 2010 demonstrates the value of teaching these skills in the early years and illustrates some of the ways that this might be done. It is a sequential body of work that offers insights and understandings for parents, teachers and those generally involved with nurturing the young.

Throughout the book emphasis is placed on nurturing social emotional competence through practical examples of intentional and purposeful scaffolding activities and how these can be used by children and families to create a harmonious platform for building personal resilience and well-being and positive relationships with family members and others in the community.

At the outset we identified children's concerns and the strategies they use to cope. We then went about developing tools to measure their coping and ways to teach coping skills. We acknowledge that to teach these life skills to children, adults need to be sharing a language that is readily understood by children. Adults are role models and they also need to have the appropriate language concepts in order to be their children's best tutors. We then incorporated these understandings into a parenting program and a social emotional curriculum for the early years. The latter has been extended to help foster and develop intergenerational skills.

Overall, the opportunities and possibilities to impact the development of young children are infinite. We hope that teachers, parents and professionals who are making an impact on the lives of young children and their families can make use of the ideas offered in this book as a springboard or stimulus for their engagement with young children. Together, as a community, we can support young children to develop an understanding of what it means to be happy and to flourish as a socially responsible member of the family and wider community.

Acknowledgements

There are many contributors to a volume such as this who need to be acknowledged. Firstly, the staff at the Early Learning Centre at the University of Melbourne where much of the developmental work has been conducted. The environment has fostered scholarship and innovation alongside the educational undertakings. The teachers have been engaged and committed to the enterprise both as teachers and facilitators of research. The children have been the beneficiaries of the teacher's enthusiasm and commitment, as have the researchers.

Since the year 2010 there have been many research students involved in various aspects of the program of research. Much of the work has been published in peer reviewed journals and the researchers are acknowledged throughout the volume where their work is cited. However, particular acknowledgements go to the team who first set about developing the COPE-Resilience program in 2016, namely, Chelsea Cornell, Neisha Kiernan, Prishni Dobee and Danielle Kaufman. Since their innovative work there have been numerous inputs and applications, most significantly by master teacher Suzana Klarin who has helped bring others on the journey with COPE-R. A more recent addition to Social Emotional Learning at the ELC has been the trans-generational program described in Chapter 8. Young children's engagement with the elderly is an exciting significant extension of the development of teaching empathy and SEL skills to young children. The champion of that program has been Sophia Stirling, whose name appears as the sole author of Chapter 8.

As we continue to progress the early years research with ongoing evaluations and adaptions of COPE-Resilience, which is being trialled in Taiwan to meet the needs of the local curriculum, we are excited at the promise of how this work can contribute to the well-being of young children and acknowledge the researchers who continue to foster innovation and adaptation.

Finally we would like to acknowledge the support from the editorial team at Routledge who have overseen this volume to completion. It has been a pleasure to work with a team of professionals who have shepherded us through the production process with ease. We are truly appreciative for their assistance.

Chapter 1

Capturing the well-being construct in the pre-school years

'When we sit around the table to have a cup of tea, it feels like we are all around the world, we hold hands and we are all friends. We are friends of each other and the world. The love heart means I love the world and be good to it'

~ *Jane, 5-year-old*

Overview

This chapter is designed to provide the theoretical framework for the chapters to follow. The concepts of health and well-being will be explored in the contemporary context of early childhood development. Key insights from Positive Psychology and a Positive Educational perspective are considered as they relate to early childhood education. It is at this point that expanding understandings of what attitudes and skills need to be developed to ensure that young children flourish. For example, translating the work around coping will be considered in the context of early childhood education from the perspective of helping teachers to support children and their parents to take an active role in developing their self-concept, resilience and positive attitudes to learning.

Health and well-being

The global context

The definition of health as 'a state of complete physical, mental and social well-being and not merely the absence of disease or infirmity', proposed by the World Health Organization (WHO, 1948) in the preamble to the Constitution has remained unamended since 1948. In doing so it incorporates total well-being under the concept of health and puts an emphasis on the individual's subjective experience rather than the objective assessment of others. The focus on social well-being recognises the important role of the environmental context in promoting well-being of individuals. Fundamental conditions and resources for health such as social justice, equitable access to education, shelter, food, stable ecosystem etc. are some of the basic pre-requisites for a secure foundation in health, particularly for children in their early years who are reliant on others for these provisions. This is akin to a mother bird building a nest for its babies: 'The twigs intertwined for the nest and the nest is where you feel safe and where you do your growing and the baby bird grows safely to an adult' ('The Nest' – ARACY, 2014).

Chapter 2 provides a more detailed look at well-being in the early years using Bronfenbrenner's ecological systems theory of development where well-being of a child is dependent on all the elements within the ecosystem in which a child resides. Well-being in children, in simple terms, means the quality of their lives. The definition of well-being, however, varies depending on the academic and professional lens, including domains of child health, policy and legal arenas, in education, research and practice (Barblett & Maloney, 2010).

The shift to the *Knowledge Age* in the 21st century brings about new patterns of practices involving a period of major social, economic and political change. One of these is the shift in focus from measuring a nation's progress solely based on economic performance-oriented goals (e.g. Gross Domestic Products) towards those that encompass social progress, quality of life and well-being such as the Gross National Happiness index in Bhutan and the Better Life Index developed by the OECD (New Economics Foundation, 2012; OECD, 2017; OPHI, 2015). A common approach to defining and measuring well-being is to consider well-being as a multi-dimensional concept. Ben-Arieh and Frones (2007a, 2007b) defined well-being in childhood as 'encompassing quality of life in a broad sense'. This means looking at well-being from different aspects of children's lives including economic conditions, peer relations, political rights and opportunities for development, with an emphasis on social and cultural variations. Since 2013, Martorano and colleagues have been developing and refining a Child Well-Being index for the United Nations Children's Fund (UNICEF). Five dimensions of children's lives have been considered: material well-being, health and safety, education, behaviours and risks, and housing and environment. The index provides a ranking order for countries according to their performance in advancing child well-being as underpinned by the framework of the Convention on the Rights of the Child (UNICEF, 1998).

National agenda on children's well-being

Consistent with global imperative to improve the health and well-being of children, countries such as the UK, US and Australia have developed national policies, frameworks and standards for children's well-being from birth (see Chapter 3 for details). For example, Australia has launched their first national plan *The Nest* action agenda in 2013 with a vision for all

Australian children and youth to achieve six outcomes: being loved and safe; having basic necessities; being healthy; learning; participating; and having a positive sense of identity and culture (ARACY, 2014). In line with this action plan were the many initiatives to track and improve the well-being and development of children in the early years. One such initiative is the Australian Early Development Census (AEDC) which provides a national measure to monitor five areas or 'domains' of early childhood development in Australia:

- physical health and well-being
- social competence
- emotional maturity
- language and cognitive skills (school-based)
- communication skills and general knowledge.

These domains are closely linked to the predictors of good adult health, education and social outcomes (AEDC, 2015). As a population-based measure, the AEDC helps communities know how their children are progressing and highlights what is working well (developmentally on track) and what needs to be improved or developed (developmentally at risk or vulnerable) to support children and their families for health and well-being.

Positive Psychology, Positive Education, well-being and coping

Well-being as flourishing

Changes brought about in the 21st century have also perpetuated the shift of the standard of mental health from what is normative to what represents optimal functioning or flourishing. What is a good life? What makes a good life? These age-old questions have been the quest for many philosophers dating back to Aristotle, who enshrine happiness as a central purpose of human life and a goal in itself. In the past two decades, empirical research in positive mental health and psychological functioning has been gaining momentum which allows Positive Psychology to establish itself as a scientific field of study that aims to identify and foster the factors and traits that enable individuals, communities and societies to prosper and flourish (Seligman & Csikszentmihalyi, 2000). Researchers such as Westerhof and Keyes (2010) proposed three core components: emotional well-being, physiological well-being and social well-being as necessary for positive mental health. Emotional well-being can be understood from two perspectives; (i) the Aristotelian Greek word – feeling good or hedonic well-being, which is characterised by the pursuit of pleasure and is generally measured using positive affect; namely cheerfulness, happiness and contentment; (ii) the pursuit of functioning well in life or eudaimonic well-being. It is the psychological well-being that is required for optimal functioning and not just the absence of psychological ill-health (Huppert & Johnson, 2010; Keyes, 2007). Psychological well-being is about having a purpose and meaning whilst social well-being is about a belief that life matters and contributing as a member of society (Westerhof & Keyes, 2010). Flourishing or thriving is described in international literature as a state where people are living within an optimal range of human functioning most of the time, that is, experiencing positive emotions, positive psychological functioning and positive social functioning (Fredrickson & Losada, 2005; Keyes, 2007). Positive Psychology emphasises the experience of positive emotions as it allows us to broaden and build our personal resources for living the good life (Fredrickson, 2001, 2004, 2013). It also emphasises the meaning and growth that we can derive from negative experiences, losses and emotions. These together allow us to build resources such as the physical, psychological, intellectual and social for the good times and for the challenging times. Therefore, Positive Psychology is intrinsically associated with well-being. As a field, it examines a range of qualities and processes such as gratitude, compassion, mindsets, strengths-based approaches and coping towards personal goals and achieving resilience, which together contribute to positive mental health and optimal functioning and well-being as illustrated in Figure 1.1.

As can be seen in Figure 1.1, Positive Psychology contributes to coping and adaptation as well as to well-being and resilience. The two-way arrows between coping, well-being and resilience highlight that each can influence the other bi-directionally.

Positive Education in the pre-school years

The development of Positive Psychology has enabled new models of intervention which aim at fostering mental health and promoting well-being in education. Seligman and colleagues in their seminal article (2009) defined Positive Education as 'education for both traditional skills and for happiness'. It is a response to the gap between what we all want for our children – happiness, positive physical and mental health – versus the traditional focus on academic achievement as a measure of success in school. It is not a focus on mental health instead of academic achievement but is a focus on mental health in order to set the stage and give students the opportunity for academic achievement. This aligns with Abraham Maslow's (1943) hierarchy of needs indicating that emotional support should be a prerequisite for higher-order functions such as learning. Positive Education is a proactive approach utilising what we have learnt from

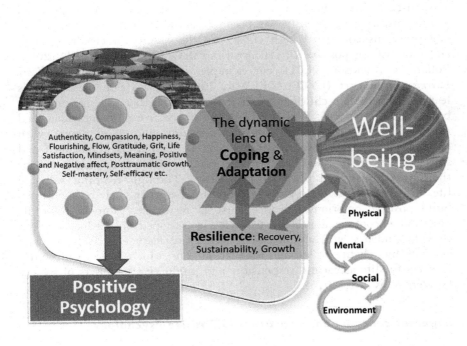

Authenticity, Compassion, Happiness, Flourishing, Flow, Gratitude, Grit, Life Satisfaction, Mindsets, Meaning, Positive and Negative affect, Posttraumatic Growth, Self-mastery, Self-efficacy etc.

The dynamic lens of **Coping** & **Adaptation**

Well-being

Resilience: Recovery, Sustainability, Growth

Physical

Mental

Social

Environment

Positive Psychology

Figure 1.1 The relationship between Positive Psychology constructs, resilience, coping and well-being

the science of Positive Psychology to teach the whole-student, that is, teaching academic skills along with mental health and well-being skills. In other words, Positive Education wants to bring Positive Psychology's goals of well-being and mental health support for not only those in distress or crisis but *everyone* into the school setting (Alford, 2017). It aims to create educational environments that enable students to engage in established curricula in addition to knowledge and skills to develop their own and others' well-being (Oades, Robinson, Green & Spence, 2011). This requires a commitment from all staff members in schools and their communities (see Chapter 9 for an example of a cross-generational community partnership to build thriving learners). Cherkowski (2018), a researcher in positive teacher leadership, proposed that teacher leadership as an 'intentional reflective process of learning to grow well-being for self and others'. This aligns with the increasing international research on the importance of well-being in schools and highlights how teachers, particularly those in leadership positions, can play a role in building collective capacity for growing well-being as central to school improvement.

Well-being in education, particularly in the early years has had a long history and recently has become central to policies, frameworks and programs concerned with enhancing the quality of children's lives and establishing positive life trajectories (McGrath, 2009; OECD, 2007; Pollard & Davidson, 2001). For example, in Australia, its *Early Years Learning Framework* (EYLF) (DEEWR, 2009) has a vision for children's learning where 'all children experience learning that is engaging and builds success for life'. Well-being is one of the five outcomes identified in the EYLF as central to children's learning and development with expectations that 'children become strong in their social, emotional and spiritual well-being', and that 'children take increasing responsibility for their own health and physical well-being'. Through teaching valuable life skills that assist early years learners to strengthen their relationships, build positive emotions, enhance personal resilience, promote mindfulness and encourage a healthy lifestyle, it is hoped that education can provide students with an increased capacity to learn effectively, as well as offering them a strong foundation on which they can build a successful life as caring, responsible and productive members of society (Waters & White, 2015).

Different concepts and constructs in Positive Psychology

What is coping?

Whilst well-being and resilience are outcomes that everyone desires or aspires to, coping is a substantive process by which it is achieved.

There are numerous definitions of coping. One widely cited description of coping is, 'conscious and volitional efforts to regulate emotion, cognition, behaviour, physiology and the environment in response to stressful events or circumstances' (Compas, Connor-Smith, Saltzman, Thomsen & Wadsworth, 2001, p. 89). The definition confirms the importance of both emotion regulation and actions in response to demands. Lazarus and Folkman (1984) defined coping as cognitive and behavioural efforts to manage specific external or internal demands that are appraised as exceeding the resources of the individual. Eisenberg and colleagues defined coping as a subset of the broader category of self-regulation in response to stress (Eisenberg et al., 1997). Substantial research in child and adolescent coping has revealed that coping is similar to adaptation with situations in which temperament, developmental and environmental factors all play a part. This means there is no right or wrong coping method but the situation determines what is likely to achieve the desired outcomes. Coping can be construed as a dichotomous dimension with both productive and non-productive coping strategies utilised in situations that individuals encounter (Frydenberg & Lewis, 2011).

It is widely acknowledged that a child's developmental level may also both contribute to and limit the type of coping responses employed and hence influence the types of coping strategies that a child utilises (Compas, 2009; Compas et al., 2001; Rudolph, Dennig & Weisz, 1995). In general, as children develop and with the increase in cortical functioning, their coping repertoire increases and shifts from primarily behavioural to more cognitive actions (Skinner & Zimmer-Gembeck, 2007). This enhances both the child's self-control when facing a stressful situation and the ability to plan effective coping options (Derryberry, Reed & Pilkenton-Taylor, 2003).

In simple terms coping can be described as the thoughts, feelings and actions in response to the demands of our everyday lives. Thoughts, feelings and actions can be articulated and, like other psychological constructs, description makes it possible for coping to be measured (see Chapter 5). Unlike many measured constructs there is no ideal score but rather a description of which strategies are used a great deal, sometimes or a little. There are good coping habits and bad coping habits. Coping fits well into the Positive Psychology frame in that we are always encouraged to upscale our use of helpful coping and downscale the use of less helpful coping strategies. Within Positive Psychology there are a range of approaches in addition to coping strategies.

Early years application

The development of the Early Years Coping Cards and their applications (see Chapter 4) highlights that children as young as three have ways to describe their coping and can learn to cope in different ways. Social learning or modelling is another way of learning about coping and children often adopt the coping styles of the adults around them. For that reason, we also want to make teachers and parents aware of coping language, described in Chapter 5, in order to best model coping to children.

Mindsets

Mindsets are core sets of beliefs that become the lenses through which individuals view, appraise and respond to the environment that they live in, which in turn influences individuals' behaviours and attitudes towards themselves and others (Dweck, 2006; Gergen, 2015; McGonigal, 2015). For example, a parent's or educator's mindset can directly influence how they feel about themselves as a learner and consequently how they feel about themselves. Similarly, a child's mindset directly affects how he or she faces challenges in the world he or she lives in. There has been extensive research to find out what mindsets would facilitate individuals to flourish. Carol Dweck (2006, 2012a, 2012b, 2015) has considered the concepts of 'growth mindsets' and 'fixed mindsets'. She described a belief system that asserts intelligence is a malleable quality and can be developed – a growth mindset. On the other hand, there is the belief that intelligence is something one is born with and the level of intelligence cannot be changed – a fixed mindset. Individuals with a growth mindset focus on *learning* – they understand that with effort and perseverance, they can succeed. On the other hand, individuals with a fixed mindset focus on *looking smart* or appearing talented as they believe that the amount of intelligence, skills or talents they have are predetermined and therefore cannot change through effort. Research shows that when children are taught to have a growth mindset, to persevere even in the face of barriers, they show an increase in not only their academic results but also their enjoyment of learning.

Early years application

Parents and educators can have a big impact on how children view themselves and they can also play a key role in helping a child to build a growth mindset that would dynamically impact their future. A good starting point is to take a step back and reflect on our own mindsets and through what specific lenses we are viewing our children. Consider the following statements:

i. Julie was born knowing her math facts.
ii. Ben just knows how to dance.
iii. Amy has always been a good child.

Although these statements sound positive, they describe who these children 'are', not the effort that they have put forth (i.e. a fixed mindset). If we give messages explicitly or implicitly that ability is fixed and ability can be measured from performance, we are very likely to undermine mastery-oriented inclinations and promote helplessness, even when the message is couched in praise. Dweck cautions us to reward children for effort rather than for achievement. Rather than saying 'you are a clever child' it is good to show recognition for the attempts and efforts that children make to do something, such as 'You really worked hard at solving that maths problem' or 'I can see you putting in good effort in putting that jigsaw puzzle together' as this is likely to encourage further effort. The message is that to maximise success we need to socialise children to see their ability as malleable and that there is a reward for effort. With growth mindsets, parents and educators believe that with effort and hard work from the learner, all children can demonstrate significant growth and therefore all children deserve opportunities for challenge. Moreover, early years educators are in the best position to differentiate and respond to each individual learner's needs, and to nurture their individual characteristics and strengths for optimum functioning. There are countless opportunities each day to teach children to love challenges, be intrigued by mistakes, enjoy effort and keep on learning.

Strengths, hope and optimism

Just as mindsets that promote well-being can be learnt and developed, so too can optimism. Learned optimism involves developing the ability to view the world from a positive point of view. It is often contrasted with learned helplessness (Seligman, 2006, 2011). By challenging negative self-talk and replacing pessimistic thoughts with more positive ones, people can learn how to become more optimistic. In one study, Seligman, Schulman and Tryon (2007) placed children with risk factors for depression in a training program where they were taught skills related to learned optimism. The results of the study revealed that children with the risk factors in the control group were much more likely to show symptoms of moderate to severe depression at a two-year follow-up. In contrast, those who had received training in learned optimism and mental health skills were half as likely to develop depressive symptoms. Studies with adults also show that optimists, that is, those with a growth mindset and positive self-efficacy, are less likely to get depressed, get fewer illnesses, have longer relationships and live longer (Carver, Scheier & Segerstrom, 2010).

Another path to well-being is the focus on fostering individual strengths (Parks & Biswas-Diener, 2013). Strengths-based approaches have been defined as intrinsically valued ways of behaving, thinking and feeling which help meet basic psychological needs for autonomy, competence and social relatedness (Linley & Harrington, 2006; Morris & Garrett, 2010). Strengths-based studies reveal encouraging findings for promoting well-being, positive relationships and successful goal achievement (Peterson & Seligman, 2004). In other words, when we focus on helping children to develop their natural abilities and personal strengths, rather than trying to improve areas of weakness, they are more likely to be motivated and have a higher level of satisfaction, feelings of mastery and competence which can then impact self-efficacy beliefs (Bandura, 1997). Some ways that parents and educators can help children to develop their strengths, hope and optimism are outlined below.

Early years application

Identifying and building strengths

Identifying a child's innate strengths and giving them opportunities to do what they do best can change the way they see themselves and the world.

Adults who can recognise their own strengths are more readily able to notice those in their child. Think of a time when you might have recognised your strengths? Could you identify moments where your child is showing those strengths (or other strengths)? How did you respond? Think of a situation in the near future where you might recognise your child's strengths – what is the situation? What is the strength? How could you encourage the use of it in different settings? For example, you can tell your child that s/he has good self-control when they are able to wait for a treat; or tell a child that they are showing great kindness when you see them comforting a crying friend. The more we help our children to identify and use their strengths, the more likely they are to develop into adults who are not only respectful but are also respected for who they truly are. Another way you can help your child to cultivate strengths would be to focus on specific strengths that have been identified by research studies as leading to positive academic and well-being outcomes such as hope, curiosity, perseverance and temperance strengths (Park & Peterson, 2009). How might you capitalise on your child's natural sense of curiosity in the day-to-day setting?

Catching the positive and building optimism

Whilst constructive criticism has its place and time, research has shown that positive reinforcement can help a child to develop self-confidence, and the confidence to tackle life's challenges and to remain positive during difficult times. Adults can help children to develop confidence, feelings of self-worth and good relationships with others by modelling positive communication. Parents can model healthy self-talk and help their child to replace negative self-talk with more productive ones. For example, when a child cries 'I can't do it, I am not good at it', parents can help them to rephrase it with the simple 'yet': 'I can't do it yet but may be if I try again tomorrow I can' or 'I have yet to develop the skills to complete this challenge'. When it comes to the ideal praise-to-criticism ratio, scientific evidence offered by Fredrickson and Losada (2005), reveals that maintaining a 3:1 positivity ratio of positive thoughts to negative emotions creates a tipping point between languishing and flourishing. We all make mistakes sometimes as humans. One way to apply the 3:1 positivity ratio in your interactions with your child could be: when you lash out at your child for breaking the cookie jar, return to them at a later time with gratitude for an opportunity to listen to them and to apologise, and for a positive and productive exchange. This does not mean we negate the negative situations, but to fill our interactions with children with more positive than negative thoughts, emotions, words and actions. Not only will we improve our relationships with our children and help them to build a sense of self-efficacy, we will also be reinforcing the type of behaviour we want to experience more from them. Having these positive interactions makes a huge difference to a child's self-efficacy. It can make all the difference between feeling optimistic and thriving or feeling disengaged. It's like the old story where a grandfather is teaching his grandson about life using the tale of two wolves. One is a good wolf which represents things like joy, peace, kindness, bravery, compassion, truth and love. The other is a bad wolf, which represents things like greed, hatred, guilt, arrogance and fear. We all have the two wolves inside us, but it is the one that we feed who wins at the end.

Grit

Grit is defined as perseverance and passion for long-term goals (Duckworth, Peterson, Matthews & Kelly, 2007). It encompasses stamina, passion or interest and effort. Only half the questions in the Grit Scale (Duckworth and Quinn, 2009) are about responding resiliently to failure. So, it is more than being resilient in the face of adversity but having a deep commitment and loyalty. Grit predicts success over and beyond talent. Therefore, it is a useful educational and training construct. Most highly successful people are both talented and gritty. Hong (2014) argues that non-cognitive character traits are more important to success, or at least as important, as cognitive abilities. There is an emphasis on character strengths like gratitude, honesty, generosity, empathy, social intelligence, tact and charisma, and being proactive. Paul Tough's 2012 book, *How Children Succeed: Grit, Curiosity and the Hidden Power of Character* emphasises that it is not so much about moral character but rather about performance character.

Duckworth, building on the work of Seligman, considered the relationship between grit and resilience, where resilience is construed as the capacity to 'bounce back' from adversity, whilst for Seligman it is more about optimism and seeing the possibilities of making changes in one's life. Grit is seen as a personality construct that identifies an individual's long-term drive and determination. Therefore, having goals and pursuits and seeing demands as challenges is associated with grit. It is a relatively recent area of study with many unanswered elements. For example, Levy and Steele (2011) consider that there is an association between grit and attachment, both in the early years and even more so in the adult years. Grit is captured in the toddler years by observing the child moving from being a crawler to one where they make attempts to stand, albeit whilst being attached to something, and then setting about to try to walk. Despite many failures the child picks him or herself up and tries again. Rewarding effort is about encouragement, saying words like 'you are almost there' and often the parent or adult stands a short distance away making it clear that they are ready to welcome or assist the child.

Early years application

Cultivating grit and self-regulation

Grit is defined as perseverance and passion toward long-term goals. Gritty people tend to be more self-regulated. Studies have found that the correlation between self-discipline and achievement is twice as large as the correlation between IQ and achievement. The basis of grit and self-regulation is developed very early as children start to play – with toys and with each other. Using play as the all-important foundation provides opportunities to teach and cultivate grit and self-regulation. Chapter 2 helps in understanding the neural basis of self-control and how to shape it through appropriate play, games, teaching methods and other activities tailored to the needs of young children.

Gratitude

Gratitude has been defined as 'a sense of thankfulness and joy in response to receiving a gift, whether the gift be a tangible benefit from a specific other or a moment of peaceful bliss evoked by natural beauty' (Emmons, 2004, p. 554). Be it feeling grateful to someone or for something that exists or happened, both have been shown to be associated with higher levels of well-being (Watkins, Woodward, Stone & Kolts, 2003). Researchers have suggested that gratitude serves a social function in helping build and maintain relationships between family members and the wider kinship group. More importantly, gratitude encourages individuals to focus their attention on the positive aspects of their life, in contrast with dwelling on negative issues and events (Emmons, 2008). The practice of gratitude serves as a deliberate reminder to shift our attention to something positive in our lives. It has also been shown to be associated with other positive constructs related to well-being such as hope, life satisfaction and more proactive behaviours towards others (McCullough, Emmons & Tsang, 2002).

Early years application

Increasing gratitude

Research suggests a child who is taught to be grateful is happier, less materialistic, better behaved, more social and physically healthier. Gratitude is one of the most valuable and important emotions we possess, and it is a virtue that anyone can cultivate. Researchers have developed many different methods people can use to foster an attitude of gratitude, and the science shows that they really do work. As we connect with gratitude, our focus shifts to what resources we have and helps keep things in perspective.

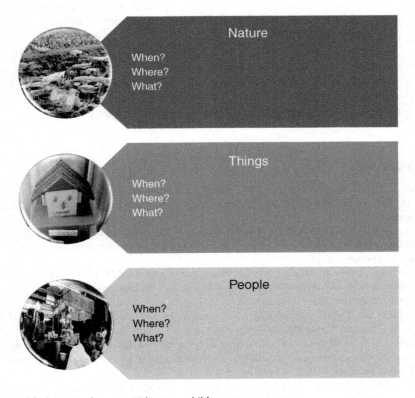

Figure 1.2 A gratitude game with young children

You can do this activity (Figure 1.2) with your children to cultivate gratitude in the simple things in everyday life.

Take home messages

- Well-being is not just the absence of ill health or disappointment; it is about experiencing positive emotions, being able to savour the moment and having satisfaction.
- Positive Psychology interventions often focus on ways to build internal strengths, gratitude and growth mindsets.
- At a child level, Positive Psychology is about bringing up children who are engaged with the world around them, who retain curiosity to explore their environment and gain satisfaction when they accomplish a task.
- We want children not only to be willing to engage in challenging activities but also to be able to engage with and relate to others, to show gratitude and to appreciate their surroundings.

- A key aspect of achieving this is through adopting a strengths-based approach, which recognises and builds upon students' inherent virtues and strengths.
- A strengths-based approach provides opportunities for students to develop their capacity to build and maintain positive relationships with others, manage their emotions and develop self-confidence and self-esteem.
- Coping skills contribute significantly to resilience and well-being.

References

Alford, Z. (2017). Positive education: developing skills for school life and beyond. In M. White, G. Slemp, & A. Murray (Eds.), *Future directions in well-being*. Cham: Springer.

Australian Early Development Census Data. (2015). Australian early development census domains fact sheet. Retrieved from www.aedc.gov.au/resources/detail/about-the-aedc-domains

Australian Research Alliance for Children and Youth (ARACY). (2014). *The Nest action agenda: Improving the wellbeing of Australia's children and youth while growing our GDP by over 7%*. Canberra: ARACY.

Bandura, A. (1997). *Self-efficacy: The exercise of control*. New York, NY, US: W H Freeman/Times Books/Henry Holt & Co.

Barblett, L., & Maloney, C. (2010). Complexities of assessing social and emotional competence and wellbeing in young children. *Australasian Journal of Early Childhood, 35*(2), 13–18.

Ben-Arieh, A., & Frones, I. (2007a). Indicators of Children's Well Being – Concepts, Indices and Usage. *Social Indicators Research, 80*, 1–4.

Ben-Arieh, A., & Frønes, I. (2007b). Indicators of Children's Well being: What should be Measured and Why? *Social Indicators Research, 84*, 249–250.

Carver, C. S., Scheier, M. F., & Segerstrom, S. C. (2010). Optimism. *Clinical Psychology Review, 30*, 879–889.

Cherkowski, S. (2018). Positive teacher leadership: Building mindsets and capacities to grow wellbeing. *International Journal of Teacher Leadership, 9*(1), 63.

Compas, B. (2009). Coping, Regulation, and Development During Childhood and Adolescence: Coping and the development of regulation. *New Directions for Child and Adolescent Development, 124*, 87–99.

Compas, B. E., Connor-Smith, J. K., Saltzman, H., Thomsen, A. H., & Wadsworth, M. E. (2001). Coping With Stress During Childhood and Adolescence: Problems, Progress, and Potential in Theory and Research. *Psychological Bulletin, 127*(1), 87–127.

Department of Education, Employment and Workplace Relations for the Council of Australian Governments (DEEWR). (2009). *Belonging, Being and Becoming: The Early Years Learning Framework for Australia*. Canberra: Australian Government.

Derryberry, D., Reed, M. A., & Pilkenton-Taylor, C. (2003). Temperament and coping: Advantages of an individual differences perspective. *Development and Psychopathology, (4)*, 1049.

Duckworth, A. L., Peterson, C., Matthews, M. D., & Kelly, D. R. (2007). Grit: Perseverance and passion for long-term goals. *Journal of Personality and Social Psychology*, 96(6), 1087–1101.

Duckworth, A. L., & Quinn, P. D. (2009). Development and validation of the short grit scale (Grit-S). *Journal of Personality Assessment*, 91(2), 166–174. doi:10.1080/00223890802634290

Dweck, C. (2006). *Mindset. The new psychology of success: How we can learn to fulfil our potential*. New York, NY: Random House.

Dweck, C. (2012a). *Mindset: How You Can Fulfil Your Potential*. New York, NY: Constable & Robinson.

Dweck, C. S. (2012b). *Mindset: How you can fuel your potential*. Great Britain: Robinson.

Dweck, C. (2015). Growth. *British Journal of Educational Psychology*, 85, 242–245. doi:10.1111/bjep.12072

Eisenberg, N., Guthrie, I. K., Fabes, R., Reiser, M., Murphy, B. C., Holgren, R., … Losoya, S. (1997). The Relations of Regulation and Emotionality to Resiliency and Competent Social Functioning in Elementary School Children. *Child Development*, 68(2), 295–311.

Emmons, R. A. (2004). The Psychology of Gratitude: An Introduction. In R. A. Emmons & M. E. McCullough (Eds.), *Series in affective science. The psychology of gratitude* (pp. 3–16). New York, NY, US: Oxford University Press.

Emmons, R. A. (2008). Gratitude, subjective well-being, and the brain. In R. J. Larsen & M. Eid (Eds.), *The Science of Subjective Well-Being*. New York, NY: The Guilford Press.

Fredrickson, B. (2001). The role of positive emotions in Positive Psychology: The broaden and build theory of positive emotions. *American Psychologist*, 56(3), 218–226.

Fredrickson, B. (2004). The broaden and build theory of positive emotions. *Philosophical Transaction of the Royal Society*, B.359, 1367–1377.

Fredrickson, B. (2013). Positive Emotions Broaden and Build. *Advances in Experimental Social Psychology* (Vol. 47). Elsevier.

Fredrickson, B., & Losada, M. (2005). Positive affect and complex dynamics of human flourishing. *American Psychologist*, 60, 678–686.

Frydenberg, E., & Lewis, R. (2011). *Adolescent Coping Scale-2*. Melbourne: Australian Council for Educational Research.

Gergen, K. (2015). *An invitation to social construction* (3rd ed.). Thousand Oaks, CA: Sage.

Hong, P. Y. P. (2014). How children succeed: Grit, curiosity, and the hidden power of character, Paul Tough. *Qualitative Social Work*, 13(3), 438–442, 435. doi:10.1177/1473325014530940a

Huppert, F. A., & Johnson, D. M. (2010). A Controlled Trial of Mindfulness Training in Schools: The Importance of Practice for an Impact on Well-Being. *The Journal of Positive Psychology*, 5, 264–274.

Keyes, C. L. M. (2007). Promoting and Protecting Mental Health as Flourishing A Complementary Strategy for Improving National Mental Health. *American Psychologist*, 62(2), 95–108.

Lazarus, R. S., & Folkman, S. (1984). *Stress, appraisal, and coping.* New York: Springer.

Levy, J. M., & Steele, H. (2011). Attachment and grit: Exploring possible contributions of attachment styles (from past and present life) to the adult personality construct of grit. *Journal of Social and Psychological Sciences, 2,* 16.

Linley, P. A., & Harrington, S. (2006). Playing to Your Strengths. *The Psychologist, 19,* 86–89.

Martorano, B., Natali, L., de Neubourg, C., & Bradshaw, J. (2013). 'Child wellbeing in advanced economies in the late 2000s', *Working Paper 2013-01.* UNICEF Office of Research, Florence. Retrieved from www.unicef-irc.org/publications/pdf/iwp_2013_1.pdf

Maslow, A. H. (1943). Conflict, frustration, and the theory of threat. *The Journal of Abnormal and Social Psychology, 38*(1), 81–86.

McCullough, M. E., Emmons, R. A., & Tsang, J. (2002). The grateful disposition: A conceptual and empirical topography. *Journal of Personality and Social Psychology, 82,* 112–127.

McGonigal, K. (2015). *The upside of stress: Why stress is good for you, and how to get good at it.* New York, NY: Penguin.

McGrath, H. (2009). *An evidence-based Positive Psychology approach to student wellbeing.* Paper presented at the 1st Australian Positive Psychology in Education Symposium, University of Sydney.

Morris, D., & Garrett, J. (2010). Strengths: Your leading edge. In P. A. Linley, S. Harrington, & N. Garcea (Eds.), *Oxford library of psychology. Oxford handbook of Positive Psychology and work* (pp. 95–105). New York, NY, US: Oxford University Press.

New Economics Foundation. (2012). *Measuring Wellbeing: A guide for practitioners.* London: New Economics Foundation.

Oades, L. G., Robinson, P., Green, S., & Spence, G. B. (2011). Towards a Positive University. *The Journal of Positive Psychology, 6,* 432–439.

OECD. (2007). *Understanding the Brain; the Birth of a learning Science.* OECD.

OECD. (2017). *How's Life? 2017: Measuring Well-being.* OECD.

Oxford Poverty and Human Development Initiative (OPHI). (2015). Retrieved from www.ophi.org.uk/wp-content/uploads/Informing-Policy-brochure-web-file.pdf

Park, N., & Peterson, C. (2009). Strengths of character in schools. In R. Gilman, E. S. Huebner, & M. J. Furlong (Eds.), *Handbook of positive psychology in schools* (pp. 65–76). New York, NY: Routledge/Taylor & Francis Group.

Parks, A. C., & Biswas-Diener, R. (2013). Positive interventions: Past, present, and future. In T. B. Kashdan & J. Ciarrochi (Eds.), *The Context Press mindfulness and acceptance practica series. Mindfulness, acceptance, and positive psychology: The seven foundations of well-being* (pp. 140–165). Oakland, CA, US: Context Press/New Harbinger Publications.

Peterson, C., & Seligman, M. E. P. (2004). *Character strengths and virtues: A classification and handbook.* New York, NY: Oxford University Press. / Washington, DC: American Psychological Association.

Pollard, E., & Davidson, L. (2001). Foundations of child well-being. In *Action Research in Family and Early Childhood Monograph Series.* Paris: UNESCO.

Rudolph, K., Dennig, M., & Weisz, J. (1995). Determinants and consequences of children coping in a medical setting: Conceptualisation, review and critique. *Psychological Bulletin, 118*(3), 328–357.

Seligman, M. E., Schulman, P., & Tryon, A. M. (2007). Group prevention of depression and anxiety symptoms. *Behaviour Research and Therapy, 45*(6), 1111–1126.

Seligman, M. E. P. (2006). *Learned optimism: How to change your mind and your life.* New York, NY: Vintage Books.

Seligman, M. E. P. (2011). *Authentic happiness. {Electronic resource}: Using the new positive psychology to realise your potential for lasting fulfilment.* London: Nicholas Brealey Publishing.

Seligman, M. E. P., & Csikszentmihalyi, M. (2000). Positive psychology: An introduction. *American Psychologist, 55,* 5–14.

Seligman, M. E. P., Ernst, R., Gillham, J., Reivich, K., & Linkins, M. (2009). Positive Education: Positive Psychology and classroom interventions. *Oxford Review of Education, 35,* 293–311.

Skinner, E. A., & Zimmer-Gembeck, J. (2007). The development of coping. *Annual Review of Psychology, 58,* 119–144.

Tough, P. (2012). *How children succeed: Grit, curiosity, and the hidden power of character.* Houghton Mifflin Harcourt.

UNICEF. (1998). *Convention on the rights of the child.* Retrieved 20 November 2018 from www.unicef.org/crc/files/Rights_overview.pdf

Waters, L., & White, M. (2015). Case study of a school wellbeing initiative: Using appreciative inquiry to support positive change. *International Journal of Wellbeing, 5*(1), 19–32.

Watkins, P., Woodward, K., Stone, T., & Kolts, R. (2003). Gratitude and happiness: Development of a measure of gratitude and relationships with subjective well-being. *Social Behavior and Personality, 31*(5), 431–451.

Westerhof, G., & Keyes, C. L. M. (2010). Mental Illness and Mental Health: The Two Continua Model across the Lifespan. *Journal of Adult Development, 17,* 110–119.

World Health Organization. (1948). Preamble to the Constitution of the World Health Organization as adopted by the International Health Conference, New York, 19–22 June, 1946; Signed on 22 July 1946 by the representatives of 61 States (Official Records of the World Health Organization, no. 2, p. 100) and entered into force on 7 April 1948.

Chapter 2

Development in context

'Coping is finding ways of how your friends can help you be good again'

~ Angel, 5- year-old

Overview

Human development is a dynamic and complex process impacted by genetic, epigenetic and environmental factors. Building on the earlier work of Lev Vygotsky (1962) and Jean Piaget (1952), Uri Bronfenbrenner's (1979) socio-ecological perspective has been widely adopted and adapted since the 1970s to explain development in context. In the last two decades neuroscience or neurobiology along with epigenetics are continuing to advance our understanding of human capability and adaptation. This chapter provides an overview of the different theories in the contemporary context of early childhood development and well-being; from the age-old debate of nature versus nurture to how genes moderate environmental influences and vice versa.

How nature and nurture interact

Development continues from conception to late adulthood. One of the oldest philosophical issues within psychology considers the relative contributions of genetic inheritance and environmental factors to human development. The unidimensional approach of nature versus nurture as being most significant developmentally has been replaced by the contemporary consensus that there is interplay between genetic predisposition and environmental opportunities. Whilst the relative contribution of each is still under discussion, it is important to acknowledge that both play a significant role in a child's progression through life. Facets of development also act in tandem or interactively, but it is helpful to focus on each of the elements individually to best understand which significant aspects of development occur year by year. It is also important to note that children vary as to when they reach their developmental milestones in one aspect of their development and there may be asynchrony in how this occurs compared to another aspect of development. For example, a child may be advanced in language and cognitive development but may not have reached a similar milestone in social emotional development. Table 2.1 identifies physical aspects of development such as gross and fine motor skills, and social emotional development, language and thinking, from 3 years through to 6.

Piaget's theory of cognitive development: an example of how nature and nurture interact

Whilst there are numerous theories of cognitive development, some more controversial than others, Piaget's Cognitive Theory is one that is most familiar to parents and educators and one that recognises the interplay between biological maturation and environmental experience in a child's cognitive development.

Piaget (1952) viewed children as active learners, in which their development and knowledge are based on their experiences and interactions with the world. The child actively constructs their understanding of their world through exploring and interacting with the environment. In addition to perceiving children as active learners, he proposed four discrete stages of child development; with each stage explaining the processes and mechanisms employed to assist the development of the child's cognitive skills.

These four stages of cognitive development include:

- Sensorimotor (birth–2 years old): The infant learns about the environment through responding to sensory stimuli through motor actions. The child acquires knowledge and understanding through physically acting with the object (e.g., looking, touching, grabbing).
- Pre-Operational (2–7 years old): Children begin to understand symbolic meaning as opposed to the physical and concrete observations made in the previous stage. During this stage, children begin to use symbols in a more organised and logical manner.
- Concrete Operational (7–11 years old): Children's thinking becomes more flexible and logical. While children's learning mainly stems through actions, their ability to think in more abstract ways increases. This stage marks the understanding that quantities remain the same even if they change in shape or are different in appearance.
- Formal Operations (11–15 years old): The child/adolescent gains the ability to think hypothetically and uses abstract ideas, resulting in a more effective manner of thinking. Adolescents are able to have conversations about abstract topics in a meaningful manner.

Table 2.1 Developmental milestones of pre-schoolers

Domains of Development	3-year-old	4-year-old	5-year-old	6-year-old
Physical and motor development	• Walks with swinging arms • Runs around obstacles without falling • Bounces a ball and catches it • Climbs ladders; uses slide independently • Rides a tricycle or bike • Balances or hops on one foot and climbs • Assembles simple puzzles or blocks • Copies and draws simple shapes and letters • Attempts to dress self	• Running is more controlled; can start, stop and turn quickly • Uses large muscles to throw, skip, catch, turn somersaults and bounce with more accuracy • Begins to pedal a two-wheeled bike with training wheels • Copies crosses, squares and paints with a paintbrush • Writes own name • Uses table utensils skilfully • Brushes teeth, combs hair, washes and dresses with little assistance	• Runs in an adult manner • Balances well – can walk on a balance beam, lines on the floor, tiptoe or broad jumps • Throws a ball to a target overhand and underhand • Learns to skate and skip rope • Shows hand dominance or preference • Grasps pencil using a three-finger grasp • Colours within lines • Starts tying their shoes	• Walk backward • Jump rope/hop proficiently • Copy simple shapes such as rectangle, triangle, circle etc. • Learning to write letters • Use scissors to cut on curved lines, cuts out shapes and simple designs • Stronger hand-eye coordination and can thread and manipulate small and large beads
Social and emotional development	• Follows simple directions; enjoys helping with household tasks	• Engages in turn taking, sharing, waiting and cooperates in group play	• Takes turns and shares more easily and are better at following simple rules	• Becomes more aware of emotions of their own and those of others • Enjoys showing off talents

	• Begins to understand some rules and own limits – asks for help • Engages in solitary and parallel play • Begins turn taking but continues the difficult task of learning to share • Makes simple choices (between two things) • Begins to notice other people's moods and feelings • Shows fear and cries easily – eager to please adults at times	• Engages primarily in associative play and likes to make friends • Increasing perspective taking skills and can read emotions and express those in words • Expresses anger verbally rather than physically • Can feel jealousy • May sometimes lie to protect him/herself, but understands the concept of lying • Increasingly inventive in fantasy play • Views self as a whole person involving body, mind and feelings	• Distinguishes right from wrong, honest from dishonest, but does not recognise intent • Shows strong emotions such as anger, excitement and anxiety • Is sensitive to the feelings of others and responds to appropriate praise • Shows strong connection to family, especially siblings • Seeks to play rather than be alone; friends are important • Plays with both boys and girls but prefers the same sex • Wants to conform; may criticise those who do not	• Peer acceptance and adults' approval are important – learning to cooperate and share • Prefers to play with peers of the same sex • More independent from family, able to dress themselves (might need help with difficult buttons) • Fears may continue to emerge (monsters, dark, falling, dogs etc.) • May exhibit habits while feeling tired, nervous, upset (nail biting, blinking, thumb sucking etc.) • Uses language to describe thinking and feeling • Focuses better in school (for 15 mins)
Language and thinking development	• Starts to understand and engage in conversation	• Speaks in relatively complex sentences (six to ten words)	• Starts constructing sentences that include	• Speaks with correct grammar most of the time

(Continued)

Table 2.1 (Cont.)

Domains of Development	3-year-old	4-year-old	5-year-old	6-year-old
	• Speaks in complete sentences of three to five words • Starts using language socially (make requests, greet others etc.) • Begins to use the basic rules of grammar • Enjoys asking questions and learning new words • Learns by doing and through the senses • Engages in pretend play with real objects as props or toys to symbolise real objects • Understands concepts of *now*, *soon* and *later*; begins to recognise cause-and-effect relationships • Identifies and names body parts with their greater memories	• Understands words that relate one idea to another – *if*, *why*, *when* • Follows three-step directions • Pronounces words and sounds correctly • Mostly understands the difference between fantasy and reality • Understands number and space concepts: *more*, *less*, *bigger*, *in*, *under*, *behind* • Begins to reason and practice problem-solving • Notices and identifies patterns and can sort or categorise them • Grasps the concepts of *past*, *present* and *future* but does not understand the duration of time • Begins to extend their play themes based on their backgrounds and interests	details and converses easily with adults • Speaks clearly and fluently with correct use of plurals, pronouns and tenses • Likes to ask a lot of questions and expresses interest in creative movements • Uses language to control activities and peers and make up stories • Understands and names opposites • Uses measurement terms such as long, heavy, whole, half etc. • Sorts and organises concrete objects easily and can count 20+ objects with accuracy • Thinking is still naive; doesn't use adult logic	• Can use more words to describe an activity or their favourite shows or stories • Starts understanding jokes and can use humour in verbal expression • Understands the concept of numbers and able to tell time and their age

Notes to facilitate learning and development

3-year-olds have a natural tendency to explore the world through all of their senses

- Prepare transitions by providing a heads up for changes such as: 'We're leaving in 15 minutes'
- Provide a sense of security through rituals, household routines and schedules
- Facilitate learning of colours and numbers by pointing them out in the course of everyday conversation
- Encourage independent activity to build self-reliance
- Provide lots of sensory experiences for learning and developing coordination: sand, mud, finger paints, puzzles.

4-year-olds are funny, silly, imaginative, energetic and often impatient – be calm with them

- Continue to nurture their love of trying new words and activities through day-to-day experiences
- Provide lots of positive encouragement as they crave adults' approval
- Display calendars and analogue clocks to help your child visualise the concept of time
- Provide opportunities for them to focus or work on tasks for a longer period of time (e.g. word games)
- Offer opportunities for sorting, matching, counting and comparing
- Provide lots of play space and occasions to play with other kids.

5-year-olds are curious by nature and excited about learning and ask questions when experiencing new situations and circumstances – learn best through play-based activities

- Encourage them to join in activities that develop coordination and balance such as skipping and hopping, walking on the kerb or cracks in the sidewalk or climbing trees
- Facilitate their interactions with peers and adults so that they could start developing an interest in the community and outside world
- Help them recognise her/his emotions by using words to describe them: 'I see you're angry at me right now'.

6-year-olds are more independent and can be quite active – remember to provide plenty of rest and a well-balanced diet for them. Help them to structure quiet-time to include quiet-time

- Reinforce mastered skills and give children opportunities to be successful in new, simple activities
- Allow and respond to child-initiated conversation and provide reassurance when child is expressing fear
- Stay calm when responding to an increase in nervous habits as it is likely to be temporary and normal. Deal with the cause of the tension rather than the habit exhibited
- Help the child learn to accept responsibility for their own actions in a positive, caring manner.

According to Piaget (1952), a child's ability to learn depends on their stage of development which allows adults to interact with children in an appropriate manner related to their cognitive developmental ability.

However, Piaget's theory underestimated young children's ability in some areas and his theory did not take into account the role individual differences, culture and education play in promoting cognitive development. Consequently, we see a more flexible progression of children through their developmental stages that is linked to the socio-cultural context.

Socio-cultural theory of development

Vygotsky (1962) laid the groundwork for the 'Socio-Cultural Theory of Development' which emphasises the social and cultural origins of development. Vygotsky considered cognitive and linguistic development as a relationship between the individual and his or her environment. To Vygotsky, language and thought worked together as a coupled process with external speech turning thoughts into words and inner speech words morphing into thoughts. In contrast, human communication is the result of social interaction. For example, pointing to an object can not only communicate the child's interest in the object but engages the adult in a communicative relationship.

The socio-cultural theory of development signals to adults ways in which they can understand and facilitate development in children to utilise the context whilst at the same time appreciating that individual differences and unique experiences play their part. Scaffolding is the means by which adults support development in that assistance is provided for a child to reach beyond their current level of performance in any task, be it language, motor or cognitive skills. For example, if support is provided for the child when he or she has accomplished a milestone such as walking, the child can be assisted to ride a tricycle to the stage where it can be performed independently with a degree of confidence. Scaffolding is a powerful contributor to a child's learning throughout the lifespan. Parents, teachers and caregivers are generally well placed to provide scaffolding so that learning can take place. The early work of Vygotsky was expanded considerably through the work of Yuri Bronfenbrenner.

The ecological approach

Throughout the late 1970s and 1980s, Bronfenbrenner (1979) proposed the model 'Ecological Systems Theory' which views human development as an interaction between the individuals and their environments. The model established a focus on the role of context in human development.

The five ecological systems for development described by Bronfenbrenner include:

- Microsystem: The individuals and institutions closest to the individual, e.g., family, school, peers, neighbourhood and church.
- Mesosystem: The interactions between microsystems, e.g., between parents and the school; between the child and the community.
- Exosystem: The structures with the microsystem that indirectly affect the young person, e.g., financial difficulties within the family may impact the child.
- Macrosystem: The culture in which the individual lives, e.g., socio-economic status, ethnicity, laws.
- Chronosystem: How a person and his/her environment changes over the life course, as well as socio-historical circumstances, such as growing gender equality.

In the mid-1980s, in response to research starting to over-emphasise context and ignore development, Bronfenbrenner presented his 'Bio-ecological Systems Theory'.

This theory is based on the Process-Person-Context-Time model:

- Process: Proximal processes or the interaction between a person and their environment as the key mechanism for development.
- Person: The role personal characteristics play on how an individual interacts with their environment and consequently their proximal processes.
- Context: The five ecological systems (as above).
- Time: The influence micro-time, meso-time and macro-time have on a person's development.

The bio-ecological systems model adds to our understanding of human development by highlighting how both the person and the environment influence one another bi-directionally and time plays a significant part in development. It is a multifaceted complex picture of development.

According to the ecological approach 'resilience is based on the complex and bi-directional transactions between individuals and their context' (Schoon, 2006, p. 19). There are nested spheres of influence depending on proximity from micro to macro or vice versa. The spheres of influence include biological disposition, family influences, lives that are interlinked and neighbourhoods, with all the associated influences. Like Schoon, Hobfoll has described the individual as nested in the family which in turn is nested in the tribe which is often expressed as community or communal coping (Hobfoll, 2001). Figure 2.1 takes account of the individual's social emotional development in the context of the family and pre-school

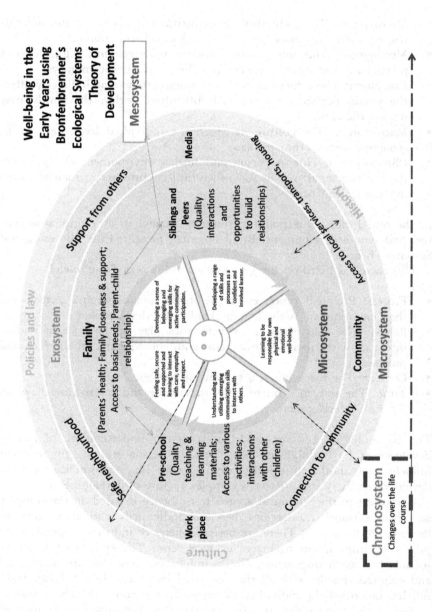

Figure 2.1 Well-being in the early years using Bronfenbrenner's ecological systems theory of development

settings. It also incorporates the broader community within which schools and families operate as well as culture and the wider policy context. There is an overlay of time along with the two-way interaction between the person and the environment. For example, where a child spends his or her time may be determined both by policy as well as the child's response to the opportunities provided from any number of sources such as from the home, school or family. Development is subsequently impacted by family practices, modelling by adults and siblings as well as a pre-school environment where there are opportunities for learning.

The developmental milestones detailed in Table 2.1 together with the complex ecological model in Figure 2.1 highlight the multiplicity of factors that are at work in the course of development. Development is not linear but interactional in multiple directions. For example, if a child is in a nurturing home environment with emotional support then it is likely that physical development may progress according to or beyond age-related expectations. Alternatively, if a child is lacking in care and support in the home setting, and is physically underdeveloped compared to peers, they may be teased and generally experience unhappiness which may further exacerbate delays in his or her social emotional and physical development. It is within this bio-ecological model that our contemporary understanding of neuroscience and epigenetics sits, in that there is a continuous interaction between persons and their environments that impacts outcomes. The synthesis between psychology and biology has been well established in that individual differences in human behaviour are significant and are determined by a host of factors, including biology and the interplay between the individual and their environments. Thus, whilst the literature on ecology and neuroscience has developed independently there is a clear intersection between the two.

Social emotional development: understandings from neuroscience and the brain development

Our understanding of development in general is continuously evolving. In particular, in recent years both neuroscience and epigenetics have contributed to the ways in which we understand child development.

Neuroscience on how the brain develops

In recent years the interest in neuroscience as a way of thinking about development and learning has come into prominence. Neuroscience or neurobiology is the study of the nervous system which includes anatomy, biochemistry, molecular biology and the physiology of neurons and neural circuits. It draws on multiple disciplines such as biology, physics, ecology and psychology. The emphasis is often on the functioning of the human brain. Whilst it continues to be a work in progress it is well accepted that brain development begins in utero and continues from birth through adolescence into adulthood.

Between childhood and adulthood, the brain's wiring becomes more complex and efficient, particularly the brain's frontal lobe which is the seat of higher order functions such as learning and socialisation (see Figure 2.2 for an illustration). The prefrontal cortex (PFC) is an important part of the frontal lobe, and is often referred to as the CEO or executive of the brain because it sets priorities, organises, plans and formulates ideas, develops strategies, controls impulses and allocates attention. It is suggested that the PFC is the last part of the brain to mature. The brain is in a dynamic biologic state and it exits each period in a different state than how it enters it. By adulthood certain connections are strengthened and others weakened. The influences are both genetic and environmental.

The maturing brain grows circuits like a computer with neural connections that can perform several tasks simultaneously with greater efficiency. Dopamine inputs to the PFC as a chemical messenger, which is critical for focusing attention when it is necessary to choose between conflicting options as the child grows older.

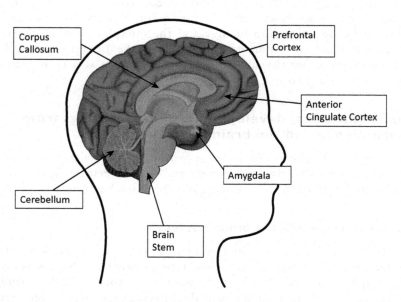

Figure 2.2 Brain parts and functions

The role of executive functioning

Executive functioning, also known as executive control, gives an individual the ability to plan, remember, focus, multitask and keep impulses in check. The pre-school years are a critical period for the development of executive function. From the ages of 3–5 pre-schoolers develop a deeper understanding of themselves, their language skills bloom and they are more adept at working towards a goal. Whilst generally executive functioning has been considered to be comprised of three distinct elements, namely, working memory which allows one to hold information, inhibitory control which allows one to ignore distractions and set shifting which is about mental flexibility, it has been suggested that in the early years rather than a three-part model there is the blending of working memory and inhibitory control as a single 'entwined' construct (Wiebe et al., 2011). Executive functioning becomes more efficient as children develop but in the pre-school years there is an overlap which needs to be recognised. This implies that both impulse control and learning need to be tackled simultaneously to facilitate this disentangling.

Self-regulation, emotion regulation and Social Emotional Learning

Humans are born with the ability to express six basic emotions, namely fear, anger, sadness, joy, surprise and disgust. These have been termed primary emotions. Secondary emotions develop from 2 years of age and they help children to evaluate their own behaviour and that of others. These emotions include self-consciousness, including shame, embarrassment, guilt, envy and pride. These have been called the social emotions because they are seen as impacting on self-concept. As children approach 2 years of age, they are able to understand themselves and they start displaying empathy and a recognition of the feelings of others. When it comes to promoting well-being through the implementation of Social Emotional Learning the capacity to recognise and manage emotions, have positive relations and make decisions are the core outcomes. Overall emotional competence is about having well developed emotional understandings and skills. It is about understanding one's own emotions and those of others. It is also about the capacity to cope with negative emotions, often termed self-regulation. Thus, in the early learning setting, whether it be in the home, school or community, both primary and secondary emotions are at play and opportunities for awareness and development need to be offered to advance the best outcomes.

Self-regulation underlies the management of thoughts, feelings and emotions. That requires a capacity to calm oneself when angry, make friends, resolve conflicts and make safe choices. One neurobiological theory of self-regulation likens the brain to a highly turned, highly trained orchestra in which the performers or parts of the brain have their own roles and functions, but the performance is built to a crescendo by the interplay of the performers. Blair and Raver (2015) call it a 'holistic connectionist' model which is explained in a hierarchical way starting from the base of the structure, the genes, to stress physiology, emotional reactivity and regulation, attention and to executive functioning. The hierarchy moves from the automatic to the volitional and genes play a part. The influences are both bottom up and top down so there is both maturation and development that moves in both directions. It is commonly accepted that neither nature or nurture act alone but rather in concert. When it comes to the teaching of SEL the general principle of neural activity is that 'neurons that fire together, wire together', a phrase coined by neuropsychologist Donald Hebb in 1949.

Furthermore, whilst not speaking directly to early childhood the relationship between behaviour and neural activity in shaping the brain is articulated convincingly by Blair and Raver (2015):

> As such, experientially induced neural activity can be understood to shape the relative strength of developing connections between brain areas in ways that lead to differences in cognitive and emotional profiles of self-regulation; that is, experience acting in concert with individual difference in genetic background and neural receptor balance is actively shaping the brain in ways that have implications for understanding self-regulation development and the ways in which SEL programming can be understood to affect not only behaviour but also the development of underlying neurobiology that supports self-regulation.
>
> (p. 69)

The examination of the relationship between structural and functional development in children's brains has been a relatively recent phenomena, mainly through the use of MRI studies. Rice, Viscomi, Riggins and Redcay (2014) looked at amygdala volume in adults and 4–6-year-olds and found that both children and adults inferred mental states from face-based tasks involving eye recognition whilst children also inferred mental states from story-based tasks. The amygdala is involved in social cognition beyond basic emotion processing. Structural maturation of the brain is related to self-regulation which in turn is linked with cognitive control, attention and executive functioning. For example, another brain development study (Fjell et al., 2012) showed that the surface area of the anterior cingulate cortex accounted for a significant proportion of children's cognitive development and properties of larger fibre connections accounted for variance in emotion regulation and impulse control. Deficits in self-regulation are often related to Attention Deficit Hyperactivity, poor learning and conduct problems.

Having the ability to self-regulate is important for a number of social and relational reasons but particularly because anger and distress impede learning. Brain functioning, particularly in the amygdala, releases hormones that influence how information is transmitted along the nervous system. The frontal lobe of the brain is relatively late to mature and that is the most rational part of our cognitions. Adults are expected to control their emotions, but aspects of emotion regulation begin developing though the early years of childhood (Arain et al., 2013; Richards & Xie, 2015). As Bruce Compas (2009) has pointed out, executive functioning continues to develop throughout childhood, partly as a result of myelination of the prefrontal areas that lasts throughout an extended period. So, while coping and emotion regulation are an important part of early years' development, these capacities continue to mature as children are required to manage increasingly complex emotions from early childhood through to adulthood.

Positive social experiences play a role in the development of emotion regulation, which in turn can impact a child's ability to cope with stress and develop behavioural control (Wilmshurst, 2008). As children grow and gain more social experience and cognitive sophistication, the social emotional pattern set in early childhood continues to be refined. In short, the brain is designed to promote emotion regulation, learning and affiliation across development. Additionally, affective behaviour reciprocally interacts with age-specific social demands and different social contexts.

All in all, we know that the brain continues to develop across the lifespan, there are individual variations in rate of development and there is a relationship between general development and the brain. When it comes to learning in both the cognitive and social emotional sense it is helpful to acknowledge the variations in brain development but given that there is a likelihood of a two-way interaction in that learning can help develop the brain, maximum input into both social emotional and cognitive aspects of learning are likely to achieve the best outcomes.

Learning can change the brain

Sometimes in psychological research we extrapolate from adult research to that of childhood. It is a way of establishing insights and possibilities by establishing hypotheses. For example, it has been variously pointed out that one of the earliest and most consistent findings in neuroscience research has been that learning changes the brain (Nechvatal & Lyons, 2013). For example, Norman Doidge (2007), in his seminal book *The Brain that Changes Itself*, demonstrated through a series of case studies how individuals with major damage to one part of the brain that was permanently impaired, such as the areas involved in speech and/or movement, were able to execute the same functions through the non-damaged part of the brain. As an example, post a motor accident, when one side of a person's brain was totally damaged, the other half was able to take over, develop, change and regenerate in remarkable ways that was often determined by necessity and learning.

The most exciting research to date following Doidge's influential contribution considers learning as an aspect of coping in the context of exposure to stress which induces neuro-adaptations that enhance emotion regulation and resilience. Nechvatal and Lyons (2013) identified 15 brain imaging studies with humans with specific phobias who had experienced post-traumatic stress disorder (PTSD) and exposed their subjects to stress exposure therapies that reduced anxiety. Most of the studies focused on functional changes in the amygdala and anterior cortico-limbic brain circuits that control cognitive, motivational and emotional aspects of physiology and behaviour and they convincingly demonstrated neuro-adaptation and functional brain changes. Whilst they point out that much remains to be learned about changes in timing, frequency and duration of stress exposure, we do know that effective interventions are possible. However, the sum total of all this research is that not only does the brain continue to develop throughout childhood, but learning can make a difference over and above development.

Something to consider

Whilst it is readily acknowledged that the brain develops throughout childhood and beyond and neuroscience has come to the fore, there are those that caution on what has to date been learned and what we can adopt as practice. We may agree about what goes on in the brain but how that is converted to learning is less clear. Are the learners active or passive in the generation of their knowledge (Raban, 2014)? Raban points out that learners need to be challenged to use both front and back cortex. Additionally, the same method does not work for every child and nothing works for everyone all the time. So, neuroscience will not replace our understandings from social science and cognitive development. Additionally, Raban points out that there is too much emphasis on the importance of critical periods, e.g., that you should learn a particular skill by a particular age. Development and learning continue throughout life. At this stage neuroscience doesn't offer guidelines for policy or practice but rather draws attention to what might be happening in the future. The focus should be more on the how rather than the when.

Coping and epigenetics: person-environment interaction

As noted by Compas (2009), the development of coping, self-regulation and emotion regulation are dependent on brain development as well as experiences encountered during development:

> It is axiomatic that the development of coping, self-regulation and emotion regulation are dependent on development in the brain and the central nervous system, as well as experiences encountered during development. Brain development both facilitates and constrains stress responses and coping at various points during childhood and adolescence. Similarly, some aspects of experience contribute to the development of coping skills, while other experiences may actually degrade or delimit the development of adaptive ways of coping.
>
> (p. 90)

The early experiences of children therefore play a critical role in the development of brain architecture. Epigenetics literally means 'above' or 'on top of' genetics. It refers to 'the ability of a cell to stably maintain one of several alternative states of gene expression over multiple cell generations, without changing the genetic sequence' (Sneppen, 2017, p. 5). It is the study of potential heritable changes when there is active or passive gene expression, which is also impacted by ecological factors. This ecological approach takes into account the interactions between persons and their environments.

Impact of adverse early experiences on lifelong development

Social adversity activates a conserved transcriptional response to adversity which is expressed through increased pro-inflammatory genes and decreased expression of antiviral and antibody-related genes (Cole et al., 2015). Some psychological resiliency factors help buffer resilience such as eudaimonic well-being, that is, having a meaning and purpose in life. In contrast, risk-factors such as social isolation or loneliness are likely to 'turn on' genes that can be deleterious to health. The study was supported by a sample of 108 community-dwelling older adults who provided blood samples (Cole et al., 2015). It is early days for extrapolation to childhood populations, although it is expected that the findings could be similar. Certainly, loneliness, for example, is a major risk for well-being at any age including early childhood where emotional neglect is often expressed in developmental lags.

There is growing evidence that external social conditions, particularly our subjective perceptions of these conditions, can influence the most basic biological processes. This is increasingly being understood within the field of epigenetics and underscored in the emerging field of human social genomics within it. It challenges 'the most fundamental belief that our molecular makeup is relatively stable and impermeable to socio-environmental influence' (Slavich & Cole, 2013, p. 331). Different genes can be 'turned on' and 'turned off' by different socio-environmental conditions.

Fredrickson et al. (2013) make the point that whilst psychological well-being has shown to forecast future physical health above and beyond that associated with current physical health and above and beyond its association with reduced levels of stress, depression and other negative affective states, the biological basis of this relationship is poorly understood. The question as to whether pleasure-focused, that is, hedonic[1] and eudaimonic well-being engage similar biological processes was examined with adults and has yet to be confirmed with children. Overall, the human genome may be more sensitive to qualitative variations in well-being than our conscious affective experiences.

Cole et al. (2015) considered the genomic mechanisms for people who experienced low versus high levels of subjective social isolation (loneliness) and they found 209 genes that were differentially expressed in low versus high lonely individuals. The researchers showed that for lonely individuals there was an under expression of genes bearing anti-inflammatory glugo-corticoid response elements and an over expression of genes bearing response elements for pro-inflammatory transcription factors. This provides a 'functional genomic explanation' for elevated risk of inflammatory disease for individuals who experience high levels of subjective social isolation and reduced supports (Fredrickson et al., 2013). Whilst the research is based on adults' studies, it seems to hold true for development across lifespan including the early years. What science tells us is that genes are vulnerable to modification in response to toxic stress, nutritional problems and other negative influences during foetal and child development. This underscores the importance of providing supportive and nurturing experiences for young children in the earliest years (National Scientific Council on the Developing Child, 2010).

Coping and development

The development of coping skills is an ongoing lifelong task as skills are acquired and new situations are tackled. Cognitive appraisal is the evaluation of a situation before embarking on a strategy to deal with it. The response, therefore, is not automatic but there is thinking involved. Perceptions of the external social environment that are subjective, that is, someone being perceived as

---

1 Hedonic (a word derived from the Aristotelian Greek word Hedemonia, meaning pleasure, is contrasted with eudaimonic well-being which derives from the Greek work Eudaimonia to flourish and is associated with doing good rather than the pursuit of pleasure)

friendly rather than hostile, appear to be more strongly related to genome-wide transcriptional shifts than the actual social-environmental conditions themselves (Slavich & Cole, 2013). What this all means is that perceptions matter. It is an affirmation of Richard Lazarus's emphasis on the importance of the appraisal process in coping theory. That is, how we perceive or see a situation as to whether it is one of stress, harm, loss or challenge is an important aspect of how we cope with a particular situation.

Emotion regulation comes into play as early as, for example, when a child is able to turn to another game when they are excluded from one. Pre-schoolers can also demonstrate emotional knowledge of others by being able to predict what a playmate, showing a certain type of emotion, will do. Four-year-olds know, for example, that an angry child is more likely to hit someone, and a happy child is more likely to share. When it comes to control, during the pre-school years children become increasingly able to control their emotion and tolerate frustration. They learn to inhibit emotions that can derail their behaviour and cope with circumstances that interfere with the immediate satisfaction of their own needs. They develop an increased awareness of self and are increasingly able to separate self from others. The balancing of personal goals with another's goal becomes easier at age 4, as cognitive and language skills begin to improve (Kopp, 2009). Finally, the importance of control in the coping process where the primary control is trying to change the situation such as asking to join in, and secondary control is about adapting or fitting in and going off to play somewhere else or with another game when rejected.

We know that development shapes every aspect of how children learn to cope. That is, at each age and stage of life children, like adolescents and adults, have to cope with different circumstances and the developmental stage determines what strategies are called into action. For example, a toy being broken may result in crying and anger towards the toy by a two-year-old but by the time a child is 4 he or she might use words to show frustration and upset and may even attempt to solve the problem by putting the toy together again. So developmental patterns in coping emerge as the child progresses through development. For example, strategies such as problem-solving, distraction, support seeking or escape come into play in different formats. With age there is also an increase in coping capacities with more self-reliance rather than reliance on adults or older siblings. That is, the way that help is sought changes. Crying is replaced by asking.

From asking children to describe how they cope with a range of age-appropriate situations such as saying goodbye, it is possible to generate hundreds of descriptions of coping which can then be grouped. Researchers such as Zimmer-Gembeck and Skinner (2011) describe these groupings as 'families' of coping. Some researchers go on to describe how these families progress through stages of development.

Problem-solving at birth to 18 months is about effort and repetition and by the pre-school years it is more purposeful, and assistance is being sought.

Comforting at birth to 18 months is about appealing to the caregiver or self-soothing and by the pre-school years it is about comforting oneself by getting a blanket or comforting object.

Distraction at birth to 18 months is about the caregiver being able to distract the child and by the pre-school years it is about behavioural distraction and just going off to do something else.

Escape at birth to 18 months is about looking away from the situation and by the pre-school years it maybe about leaving the situation.

Information seeking at birth to 18 months is about observation and by the pre-school years it is about asking for information directly.

There are numerous ways of defining coping and the various elements that are relevant. Coping was described in Chapter 1 as the thoughts, feelings and actions in response to particular concerns or situations. Children respond in an age-appropriate manner as highlighted by Zimmer-Gembeck and Skinner (2011). Like adults, children assess a situation as one of stress or harm or challenge, asking the question, do I have the strategies to cope?

Figure 2.3 illustrates the appraisal process in the context of coping. Additionally, it highlights the role of a parent providing scaffolding to a child

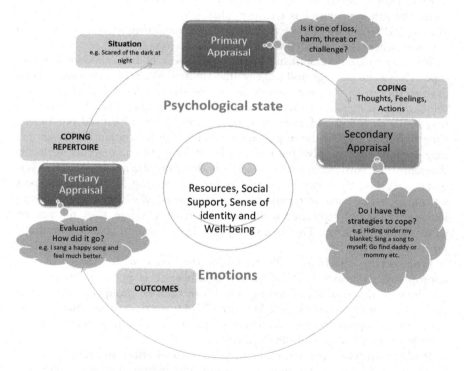

Figure 2.3 Early years appraisal process

learning to cope with fearing the dark. In the first instance the child would assess the situation as one of fear, harm ('what will happen if something scary appears?') or challenge ('I am not afraid of the dark because I can sing myself a happy song and I have my father and mother to help me cope'). When there is success it reinforces the coping strategy, such as thinking positively with the support of an adult, which was used in this situation.

Whilst our focus on coping research is on the thoughts, feeling and actions as they provide the 'best way in' with which to work with children, development plays a part as does genetics and heredity. Nevertheless, it is clear from both neuroscience and epigenetic research that environment matters and that there is an interplay between individuals and their environments.

Take home messages

- Environment matters.
- Teaching and learning can change the brain.
- Respond to the child where they are at.
- Provide the scaffolding to create opportunities to maximise the potential for development.

In Chapter 5 the descriptions of adult and child coping are detailed as derived from our research with parents, teachers and children. How these insights are translated into clinical and educational practice are dealt with in subsequent chapters.

References

Arain, M., Haque, M., Johal, L., Mathur, P., Nel, W., Rais, A., ... Sharma, S. (2013). Maturation of the adolescent brain. *Neuropsychiatric Disease and Treatment, 9*, 449–461.

Blair, C., & Raver, C. C. (2015). The neuroscience of SEL. In J. A. Durlak, C. E. Domitrovich, R. P. Weissberg, & T. P. Gullotta (Eds.), *Handbook of social and emotional learning: Research and practice* (pp. 65–80). New York: The Guilford Press.

Bronfenbrenner, U. (1979). Contexts of child rearing: Problems and prospects. *American Psychologist, 34*, 844–850.

Cole, S. W., Levine, M. E., Arevalo, J. M. G., Ma, J., Weir, D. R., & Crimmins, E. M. (2015). Loneliness, eudaimonia, and the human conserved transcriptional response to adversity. *Psychoneuroendocrinology, 62*, 11–17. doi:10.1016/j.psyneuen.2015.07.001

Compas, B. (2009). Coping, regulation, and development during childhood and adolescence: Coping and the development of regulation. *New Directions for Child and Adolescent Development, 124*, 87–99.

Doidge, N. (2007). *The brain that changes itself: Stories of personal triumph from the frontiers of brain science.* New York: Viking.

Fjell, A. M., Walhovd, K. B., Brown, T. T., Kuperman, J. M., Chung, Y., Hagler, D. J., ... Akshoomoff, N. (2012). Multimodal imaging of the self-regulating developing brain. *Proceedings of the National Academy of Sciences of the United States of America, 109*(48), 19620–19625.

Fredrickson, B. L., Grewen, K. M., Coffey, K. A., Algoe, S. B., Firestine, A. M., Arevalo, J. G., ... Cole, S. W. (2013). A functional genomic perspective on human well-being. *Proceedings Of The National Academy Of Sciences Of The United States Of America, 110*(33), 13684–13689.

Hebb, D. O. (1949). *The organization of behavior: A neuropsychological theory*. New York: Wiley.

Hobfoll, S. E. (2001). The influence of culture, community, and the nested-self in the stress process: Advancing conservation of resources theory. *Applied Psychology: An International Review, 50*(3), 337–370.

Kopp, C. B. (2009). Emotion-focused coping in young children: Self and self-regulatory processes. *New Directions for Child and Adolescent Development, 2009* (124), 33–46.

National Scientific Council on the Developing Child. (2010). *Early Experiences Can Alter Gene Expression and Affect Long-Term Development*: Working Paper No. 10. Retrieved from www.developingchild.harvard.edu

Nechvatal, J. M., & Lyons, D. M. (2013). Coping changes the brain. *Frontiers in Behavioral Neuroscience, 7*, 13.

Piaget, J. (1952). *The origins of intelligence in children*. New York, NY: W.W. Norton & Co.

Raban, B. (2014). Brain research and early childhood education: Directions that could lead us astray. *Australian Educational Leader, 36*(4), 50.

Rice, K., Viscomi, B., Riggins, T., & Redcay, E. (2014). Amygdala volume linked to individual differences in mental state inference in early childhood and adulthood. *Developmental Cognitive Neuroscience, 8*, 153–163.

Richards, J. E., & Xie, W. (2015). Brains for all the ages: Structural neurodevelopment in infants and children from a life-span perspective. *Advances in Child Development And Behavior, 48*, 1–52.

Schoon, I. (2006). *Risk and resilience: Adaptations in changing times*. Cambridge: Cambridge University Press.

Slavich, G. M., & Cole, S. W. (2013). The emerging field of human social genomics. Clinical psychological science. *A Journal Of The Association For Psychological Science, 1*(3), 331–348.

Sneppen, K. (2017). Models of life: Epigenetics, diversity and cycles. *Reports on Progress In Physics, 80*(4). doi:10.1088/1361-6633/aa5aeb

Vygotsky, L. S. (1962). *Thought and language*. Cambridge, MA: MIT Press.

Wiebe, S. A., Sheffield, T., Nelson, J. M., Clark, C. A. C., Chevalier, N., & Espy, K. A. (2011). The structure of executive function in 3-year-olds. *Journal of Experimental Child Psychology, 108*, 436–452.

Wilmshurst, L. (2008). Abnormal child psychology: A developmental perspective. *Abnormal Child Psychology: A Developmental Perspective*, 1–648. doi:10.4324/9780203893258

Zimmer-Gembeck, M. J., & Skinner, E. A. (2011). The development of coping across childhood and adolescence: An integrative review and critique of research. *International Journal of Behavioral Development, 35*, 1–17. Supplementary material.

Chapter 3

Social Emotional Learning (SEL) in the early years curriculum

'People listen to you better when you are kind and speak softly'

~ William, 4-year-old

Overview

As Social Emotional Learning (SEL) is central to early years curriculum, this chapter considers how Australian and international curriculum frameworks describe teaching and learning in this central area of child development. SEL programs are designed to help children gain self-awareness, regulate emotions, manage stress, solve problems responsibly and contribute to the wider community. These include focusing on being mindful of others and the importance of developing understandings of the perspective of others especially in relation to enacting respectful, non-judgemental and tactful attitudes. The chapter contrasts policy approaches, introduces a generic whole school systemic approach, as well as identifying a range of programs that are utilised in various communities across the globe.

The educational context: standards and definitions

Numerous inter-related terms have been used to identify what social and emotional learning (SEL) consists of (Halberstadt, Denham & Dunsmore, 2001) and generally these terms have not been defined with consistency or clarity. This chapter begins with a brief summary of how the term 'social and emotional learning' is defined across the Australia, UK and USA communities.

McKown (2015), borrowing from Lipton and Nowicki (2009), states:

> Social-emotional learning involves comprehension of social-emotional information, including encoding, interpreting, and reasoning ... [It] also involves the execution of goal-directed behaviours in interpersonal contexts.

(p. 322)

He also states that while all the theories in the field recognise that comprehension and execution are intimately related, some children have the former skills but not the latter. In other words, assessment of acquisition and performance, whilst related, are not the same (Elliott, Frey & Davies, 2015).

The Collaborative for Academic, Social and Emotional Learning (CASEL, 2013) defines SEL as:

> [T]he process by which children and adults acquire the knowledge, attitudes and skills to recognise and manage their emotions, set and achieve positive goals, demonstrate caring and concern for others, establish and maintain positive relationships, make responsible decisions [and] handle inter-personal situations effectively.

Australian Curriculum, Assessment and Reporting Authority's (ACARA, 2012) documentation refers to SEL in these terms:

> Students develop personal and social capability as they learn to understand themselves and others, and manage their relationships, lives, work and learning more effectively. This capability involves students in a range of practices including recognising and regulating emotions, developing empathy for and understanding of others, establishing positive and respectful relationships, making responsible decisions, working effectively in teams and handling challenging situations constructively.

There are several important common elements in these definitions. First, social and emotional learning consists of acquiring knowledge and developing skills. That implies the existence of two dimensions in SEL education: a cognitive dimension and a practical dimension. Like Elliott et al. (2015), McKown (2015) also noted that the acquisition of cognitive capacity (knowledge) does not necessarily mean that a person will exercise good practice (skills). It is in this gap between knowledge and skills that a third dimension, identified by CASEL, may prove decisive: attitude.

The CASEL researchers (2013) identified five core competencies to aim for in social and emotional education:

- Self-awareness
- Social awareness
- Self-management
- Relationship skills
- Responsible decision-making

Table 3.1 Social emotional learning standards and definitions in Australia, USA and the UK

AUSTRALIA		USA		UK	
ACARA (2012) Area[1] Description	Four interrelated elements of the personal and social capability learning continuum	CASEL (2013) Area[2] Description	Five interrelated sets of cognitive, affective and behavioural competencies	SEAL (2007–2011) Area[3] Description	SEAL is designed to promote the development and application to learning of social and emotional skills that have been classified under the five domains proposed in Goleman's (2005) model of emotional intelligence
Self-awareness	Developing personal and social capacities to: • recognise emotions • recognise personal qualities and achievements • understand themselves as learners • develop reflective practice.	Self-awareness	The ability to accurately recognise one's emotions and thoughts and their influence on behaviour (strengths and limitations). To develop a sense of confidence and optimism.	Self-awareness	Knowing and valuing myself and understanding how I think and feel so we can learn more effectively and engage in positive interactions with others.
Self-management	Regulating emotional responses and to work independently. Students are to:	Self-management	The ability to regulate one's emotions, thoughts and behaviours effectively in different situations	Self-regulation (managing feelings)	Developing strategies to cope with difficult emotions and to express feelings in a positive

(Continued)

Table 3.1 (Cont.)

AUSTRALIA	USA	UK
• express emotions appropriately • develop self-discipline and set goals • work independently and show initiative • become confident, resilient and adaptable.	and for working toward achieving personal and academic goals.	way so one can build better relationships and work more cooperatively and productively with others.
Social awareness Learning to show respect for and understand others' perspectives, emotional states and needs: • appreciate diverse perspectives • contribute to civil society • understand relationships.	**Social awareness** Being able to recognise social support and to take the perspective of and empathise with others from diverse backgrounds and cultures.	**Empathy** Understanding others' thoughts and feelings and valuing and supporting others – working with and learning from people from diverse backgrounds.
Social management Learning to interact effectively and respectfully with a range of adults and peers; developing the ability to initiate and manage successful personal relationships, and participate in social and communal activities: • communicate effectively • work collaboratively	**Relationship skills** Building communication, negotiation and conflict management skills. And able to seek and offer help to others.	**Social skills** Building and maintaining relationships and solving problems. For example, learning to reduce negative feelings and distraction in learning situations, and using social

		relationships as an important way of improving our learning experience.
• make decisions • negotiate and resolve conflict • develop leadership skills.	Responsible decision making	Learning to evaluate the consequences of one's behaviour – to make constructive and respectful choices about personal behaviour and social interactions. Being considerate to the well-being of self and others.
	Motivation	Approaching learning situations in a positive way – being persistent, respond effectively to setbacks and work out effective strategies for reaching set goals.

1 Australian Curriculum, Assessment and Reporting Authority (2012). General Capabilities. Retrieved from www.australiancurriculum.edu.au/GeneralCapabilities/personal-and-social-capability/organising-elements/organising-elements.
2 Collaborative for Academic, Social and Emotional Learning (2013). Social and Emotional Learning Core Competencies. Retrieved from www.casel.org/social-and-emotional-learning/core-competencies.
3 Department for Children, Schools and Families (2007). Social and emotional aspects of learning for secondary schools: tools for monitoring, profiling and evaluation. Nottingham: DCSF Publications.

ACARA adopted a similar list in the Australian Curriculum:

- Self-awareness
- Self-management
- Social awareness
- Social management

The vast majority of the most relevant work in the social emotional domain is happening in the United States (CASEL) and the United Kingdom (Social and emotional aspects of learning; SEAL). Australian initiatives such as KidsMatter are less well represented in the literature, but are nevertheless widely used in Australia and have been subjected to various evaluations. It offers possibilities of broad-spectrum cultural shifts and skill development beyond single program impacts. Table 3.1 provides a comparative table of key SEL terms used in various jurisdictions. Generally speaking, then, SEL in the context of education refers to students' development and acquisition of skills to become more aware of their emotions and how to manage them so that they can make the most of their own lives by making responsible decisions, working towards their goals, and developing respectful and fulfilling relationships with peers and adults.

Table 3.1 identifies different aspects of SEL from ACARA, CASEL and SEAL.

Table 3.1 contrasts the Social Emotional Learning areas identified by ACARA in Australia, CASEL in the USA and SEAL in the United Kingdom. It highlights the similarities and differences across the three communities both in labelling the skill areas and how the areas are described. For example, self-awareness is labelled and dealt with in much the same way by ACARA, CASEL and SEAL[4] whilst self-management is both about emotional management and stress management for ACARA and CASEL but for SEAL it is more about emotional regulation. Whilst social awareness is the term used by ACARA and CASEL, SEAL uses the term empathy. However, the application is much the same, as are the terms social management, social skills and relationships. Finally, CASEL focuses on responsible decision making and SEAL addresses motivation.

Worth considering is the point made by Weare and Gray (2003) that there is no definitive list of what constitutes emotional and social competence. They assembled a description of what it might consist of, noting that there were huge natural and social differences between people, and great variations in what was acceptable in different cultures. They nonetheless offered this list (see Table 3.2).

---

4 Whilst SEAL targets adolescents in the main its impact on policy has had reach across the entire educational sector.

Table 3.2 Elements of emotional and social competencies drawing on the work of Weare and Gray (2003)

Domain	Elements
Emotional competence	**Having self-esteem** – valuing and respecting oneself.
	Having an accurate and positive self-concept – knowing one's strengths, weaknesses, preferences and needs.
	Autonomy – thinking independently and critically.
	Experiencing a full range of emotions – recognising and understanding emotions.
	Expressing feelings – using appropriate facial expression, body language and gestures.
	Controlling emotions – recognising triggers for emotions and learning ways to cope (self-regulation).
	Increasing emotional intensity and frequency – finding and building joys and other positive emotions in life.
	Being resilient – able to bounce back and learn from experiences.
	Using information about the emotions to plan and solve problems.
Domain	**Elements**
Social competence	**Empathy** – taking perspective and understanding others' feelings.
	Communicating effectively – express one's honest feelings whilst respecting others'.
	Managing relationships – through creating trust and learning ways to manage conflicts.

Educational settings are increasingly being required to provide students with opportunities to not only grow academically, but also to become resilient, caring and productive members of society (Waters & White, 2015). The call to embed SEL in the classroom in school settings is gaining traction. Primary schooling is increasingly considered the prime intervention period as many mental health conditions are precipitated during high school (Schaps & Battistich, 1991). However, less focus has been given to the seminal development of social and emotional competencies during early childhood (Cornell et al., 2017). The opportunity for early socialisation of skill development is key, as pre-school is the first time for many children that structured social demands are placed on the child outside of the immediate home environment.

SEL as a basis for early years curriculum

Given the growing evidence and appreciation that SEL is an important component of development, the CASEL framework from the USA and related concepts for social and emotional competencies has been incorporated into the early years curriculum guidelines in the international landscape.

Australia and New Zealand

The Australian Government's *Belonging, Being and Becoming* in the early years framework contains five core learning outcomes that speak to SEL development in pre-school children; 'children have a strong sense of identity, children are connected with and contribute to their world, children have a strong sense of well-being; children are confident learners, and children are effective communicators' (Commonwealth of Australia, 2009, p. 8). The New Zealand curriculum articulates 'Children are supported to be confident and competent learners' (ERO, 2011).

What is common to these documents is the recognition of the individual and the opportunities that they need to be afforded in terms of relationship building, belonging and the importance of community.

United Kingdom

The UK Curriculum (EYFS Statutory Framework, 2017) articulates the area of personal social and emotional learning and development;

> **Personal, social and emotional development** *involves helping children to develop a positive sense of themselves, and others; to form positive relationships and develop respect for others; to develop social skills and learn how to manage their feelings; to understand appropriate behaviour in groups; and to have confidence in their own abilities*
>
> (p. 8)

> *'There is an ongoing judgement to be made by practitioners about the balance between activities led by children, and activities led or guided by adults'*
>
> (p. 9)

The areas to focus on are detailed in the section on personal, social and emotional development, namely;

Self-confidence and self-awareness: children are confident to try new activities and say why they like some activities more than others. They are confident to speak in a familiar group, will talk about their ideas and will choose the resources they need for their chosen activities. They say when they do or don't need help.

Managing feelings and behaviour: children talk about how they and others show feelings, talk about their own and others' behaviour, and its consequences, and know that some behaviour is unacceptable. They work as part of a group or class and understand and follow the rules. They adjust their behaviour to different situations and take changes of routine in their stride.

Making relationships: children play co-operatively, taking turns with others. They take account of one another's ideas about how to organise their activity. They show sensitivity to others' needs and feelings and form positive relationships with adults and other children. Before the age of 5 each child receives an EYFS Profile which is shared with parents and carers. (EYFS Statutory Framework, 2017, p. 11)

Europe and beyond

Eight countries, namely, Chile, the Czech Republic, Denmark, Estonia, Italy, Poland, the Russian Federation and the United States participated in the first phase of the Early Childhood Education Study (ECES). Whilst policy uniformities were reported there were variations. Generally, when it came to Early Childhood Education (ECE) expected outcomes, they were broad and included cognitive and non-cognitive learning outcomes, such as socio-emotional development, executive functioning and child well-being (Bertram & Pascal, 2016).

Building strong foundations in the early years

The benefits of SEL have been convincingly demonstrated both in terms of academic and socio-economic outcomes (Durlak, Weissberg, Dymnicki, Taylor & Schellinger, 2011). Even prior to Durlak et al.'s convincing data having been made available there have been curriculum requirements in the early years settings that have been made explicit, albeit requiring elaborations and detailing so as to facilitate classroom practice.

Social and emotional development during pre-school years

During the pre-school years children aged 3–6 years old undergo a period of rapid social and emotional changes. This is a critical stage in terms of increased social interactions and awareness of others, and children will gradually learn to differentiate their own needs from those of others (Thompson, Goodvin & Meyer, 2006). Social and emotional skills developed by children during this time include learning how to effectively identify and manage their emotions and build and maintain positive relationships with others

(Bierman & Motamedi, 2015). Children from a very young age can also attune to the mental states of other people and come to develop a 'theory of mind' that others' beliefs and desires may differ from their own (Thompson et al., 2006). As such, early learning settings and kindergartens can play a central role in facilitating the development of early social and emotional competencies.

As described in Chapter 2, neurologically, the period of 3 to 7 years is marked by sizeable growth in the prefrontal cortex of the brain (Diamond, 2002). This area is implicated in self-regulation skills and executive functioning; with corresponding skills in affect regulation developing across childhood and maturing during adolescence (Macklem, 2008). The ability to exert self-control is also essential for classroom and academic success. Children with higher executive functioning skills in terms of inhibition and planning show greater learning in both mathematics and reading (Bull, Espy & Wiebe, 2008). Prefrontal cortex and anterior cingulate cortex (refer to Figure 2.2 in Chapter 2 for *Brain parts and functions*) development is similarly implicated in higher order cognitions such as empathy, with interconnectivity between the prefrontal cortex and deeper neural structures including the fear-response centre of the brain, the amygdala, which is required for perspective-taking and moral decision making (Decety, Bartal, Uzefovsky & Knafo-noam, 2015).

Importantly, due to the rapid neurological development in the first five years of life, brain development is more vulnerable to environmental influence during this period (O'Shea, 2005). Neuroscience has affirmed that conditions of stress, trauma or poverty lead to experience-dependent neural and behavioural adaptation (Blair & Raver, 2016). However, less focus has been given in the literature as to the effect of positive early interventions on children's neurodevelopment (Cicchetti & Blender, 2006). Early childhood is a period of malleable neurobiology and research indicates that enriched social, emotional and learning environments can assist to overcome early adversity (Fox, Levitt & Nelson, 2010). As brain development is not passive, but an active and interactive process, it is important to consider how early intervention may also serve to build neurological resources. It is conceivable that research will one day also affirm the link between neurological trajectory of enriched social and emotional learning environments and behavioural and emotional outcomes.

Pre-school SEL programs: research and applications

As the growing awareness of the benefits of SEL has been translated into curriculum initiatives, convincing evidence has emerged from a meta-analysis of school-based universal intervention programs on significant positive effects on targeted social emotional competencies and attitudes about self and others (Durlak et al., 2011). The authors investigated 2,013 school-based programs involving 270,034 kindergarten through to high school students. When they compared these students to their controls, they reported 11 percentile points gain in achievement. Multiple outcomes, including social emotional skills, attitudes towards the self and others, positive social behaviour, conduct problems, emotional distress and academic performance in the context of interventions for the entire student body were addressed. Criteria that were considered included whether the program was Sequenced, Active, Focused and Explicit, that is, targeting specific skill sets. They used the acronym SAFE, which is really a good way of considering programs of instruction. The programs significantly improved students' skills, attitudes and behaviours.

The programs in Australia, the United Kingdom and the United States have been developed in response to the call for SEL to be incorporated into classroom practice have some core elements. In the first instance they are underpinned by a focus on social cognitions, social information processing, a focus on emotions, self-regulation and reliant on models of attachment between the teacher and the student (Bierman & Motamedi, 2015). Children learn social behaviour by observing, imitating and responding to instruction and obtaining feedback. The target skill is taught, opportunities for behavioural rehearsal are provided and there is both feedback and reinforcement. Bierman and Motamedi also describe the social information processing that occurs when children both encode information and take on board social cues to problem solve. Most programs have emotion knowledge and practices that include self-regulatory processes. They also argue that teacher–child attachment in a safe, caring environment are the means by which children learn to relate to others.

Others concur with the findings when examining early childhood programs more specifically. Rather than conducting a comprehensive meta-analysis, Bierman and Motamedi (2015) report a number of programs that work. Interestingly they found no programs that do not work in some helpful way. Thus, making the point that when there is a focus on the social emotional well-being components of education some benefits will accrue. Generally, SEL implementation requirements are articulated in curriculum documents but implementation occurs in diverse ways, ranging from unscripted whole-school approaches to scripted targeted programs for students in a particular age group.

Current social and emotional learning programs

A range of social emotional programs have emerged in response to the growing appreciation of the benefits of SEL and the curriculum requirements that have been articulated in various jurisdictions.

Apart from KidsMatter (2016) which is an exemplar of an overarching program that engages school staff to focus on early years and then recommends programs to be used, the common feature of all these programs is that they are of substantial duration that range from five sessions over five weeks to a full year. Some programs are scripted, and others are integrated into classroom practice. Each program has a unique focus or emphasis. The programs have been evaluated in diverse ways.

KidsMatter Early Childhood

KidsMatter Early Childhood (2012) is an Australian national initiative focusing on children's mental health and well-being in early childhood education and care services. It is considered to be a health promotion and prevention service which provides settings with training and resources underpinned by the National Quality Standard (Australian Children's Education and Care Quality Authority, 2018) and the Early Years Learning Framework (Commonwealth of Australia, 2009). It focuses on building relationships with an aim of developing children's social and emotional well-being and competence. There are four components: *Component One* focuses on creating a sense of community through working with parents and carers, *Component Two* focuses on developing children's social and emotional skills and is based on the fact that warm, responsive and trusting relationships between children and staff provide a foundation that allows children to learn and develop social and emotional skills through the practise of social and emotional skills in their daily interactions with staff and peers. *Component Three* focuses on children's social and emotional skill development opportunities by building a culture of partnership between staff, parents and carers. It aims to connect parents to support services and families to connect with each other. Parents are supported by access to high-quality parenting resources.

Finally, *Component Four* focuses on helping children who are experiencing mental health difficulties. This is an area where the authors comment that early childhood educators traditionally may feel out of their depth. KidsMatter Early Childhood provides the tools and resources to support services in assessing children's strengths and focusing on areas for further action. The initiative gives educators the understanding about mental health to recognise and respond to early signs of difficulty and the confidence to seek help for children and families. Staff need to have an understanding of mental health difficulties in early childhood, including common signs and symptoms, its impact on children and families, and factors that put children at risk, and to be able to respond to children who may be experiencing mental health difficulties. There are protocols and processes for recognising and responding to children who may be experiencing mental health difficulties. The service has working relationships and clear referral pathways with support services.

KidsMatter Early Childhood launched its service in 2012. The program affirms the philosophy of Positive Psychology and focuses on birth to 5 years. There are extensive resources available both online and in hard copy which are provided to services committed to implementing the initiative. The resources include PDF work books, flow charts, self-assessment tools, posters, online professional learning tools, resources for parents, professional learning guides to support parents and families with mental health issues and guides to identify children with mental health issues. Thus, it is a framework and a source of support and resources for teachers, carers and parents. The focus is less on well-being of the individual than building early childhood service and community capacity in response to mental health and well-being. There is a specific focus on connectedness, resilience, emotional literacy and community capacity. As with the KidsMatter Primary, the precursor to this program, there is an evaluation. Since this is a government funded program with support from Early Childhood Australia and Beyond Blue, and which was developed in collaboration with the Australian Psychological Society, it is a well-supported initiative with likely longevity in the early childhood and education communities.

The comprehensive 'whole of setting' approach has been evaluated (Littlefield, Cavanagh, Knapp & O'Grady, 2017) and a follow-up study conducted two years later where one in six children with mental health difficulties were found to have improved (Slee et al., 2012).

Targeted programs

In general the SEL programs targeted at enhancing pro-social skills in preschool aged children have the ability to promote positive developmental outcomes, such as positive peer relationships, reduction in externalising problems such as physical aggression, and enhanced emotional regulation (Carreras et al., 2014; Flook, Goldberg, Pinger & Davidson, 2015; Frydenberg, Deans & Liang, 2014; Myers, 2000; Smith, 2013). Common foundation skills covered in SEL programs include understanding emotions in oneself and others; caring for oneself and others and learning to be a good listener and a good communicator (Durlak et al., 2011). An early childhood environment in which children can express healthy emotions, regulate them and understand the emotions of self and others, all add up to a successful pre-school experience and also help children to cultivate empathic capacity (Denham, Bassett & Zinsser, 2012). Empathy is described as individuals being able to understand and interpret the behaviour of others, anticipate what someone else might do and feel and then respond to them (Allison, Baron-Cohen, Wheelwright, Stone & Muncer, 2011; Baron-Cohen & Wheelwright, 2004). The establishment of empathetic behaviours is considered to be important for moral reasoning and overall pro-social behaviour (Decety, 2011; Feshbach & Feshbach, 2009). Baron-Cohen and Wheelwright distinguish the cognitive from the emotional dimension of empathy. While cognitive empathy comprises emotion recognition and perspective taking, emotional empathy includes the phenomena of shared feelings more adequately to another person's situation than to one's own. A more recent study revealed that emotional empathy development is complete in the pre-school years whereas cognitive empathy develops well into the school years (Schwenck et al., 2014).

Young children (4–7 years of age) are not only competent thinkers and communicators about their own emotions and the emotions of others, but they also have the capacity for deep reflection and develop complex arguments around emotions when given conversational prompts and guided by more competent partners (Mortari, 2011). Children can learn helpful coping skills through modelling by adults, and interactions with adults and children (Frydenberg et al., 2014). In the educational context, this can be achieved through direct teaching and the use of visual tools, one example of which are 'The Early Years Coping Cards' (Frydenberg & Deans, 2011). Chapter 4 provides examples of the use of Early Years Coping Cards in role-plays and games that depict issues of concern to children and how they might deal with them.

While the content and tools/resources that constitute an SEL program in a pre-school setting are important, a less frequently considered topic in this arena is the paramount role that teachers play and their capacity to follow specifically designed programs and scaffold children's learning throughout the process of implementation of such programs. The literature notes that the connection between early years teachers' embodiment of and implementation of SEL curriculum and the development of social and emotional competence of young children is strong (Burdelski, 2010; Dachyshyn, 2015; Rosenthal & Gatt, 2010). Moreover, the stability and security of the teacher (adult) learner (child) relationship directly influences SEL (DeMeulenaere, 2015; Eisenberg, Cumberland & Spinrad, 1998). Teachers have also been identified as playing a pivotal role in enhancing SEL skills in children by creating a safe teaching and learning environment for cultivating and expressing emotions, modelling and developing empathic behaviours, encouraging and facilitating productive coping, problem-solving skills, shaping effective communication behaviours through positive reinforcement and, most importantly, weaving SEL into the school day and embodying SEL concepts moment-by-moment (Caselman, 2007; Miyamoto, Huerta & Kubacka, 2015; Rafaila, 2015).

The COPE-R program

The COPE-R program, which is detailed in classroom practice in Chapter 8, was developed in 2016 and has been implemented over a number of years in the Early Learning Centre at the University of Melbourne. Details about the implementation experience and ways in which SEL has been implemented and can be adapted in an early years setting are described and illustrated in Chapter 8. The COPE-R Program contains five sessions that emphasise Care, Open-communication, Politeness and Empathy, with sessions allocated for Review (see Table 8.1 for program details in Chapter 8). It is delivered by the teacher in large group-learning situations over a five-week period with approximately 45 minutes dedicated to each session. The COPE-R program has been integrated into the classroom curriculum and from the outset it was defined and influenced by an ecologically oriented thread (environmental key) that emerged as an outcome of interest driven curriculum (DEEWR, 2009) focusing on collectivity, connectedness and the common spirit of the group. The teacher may establish a 'community of learners' (Rogoff, 1994) by engaging the children in a range of modalities such as role-playing, meditation, singing and visual art to focus their attention on the specialised content and to maintain their interest over time (Pianta, La Paro & Hamre, 2008).

Other programs that work

Numerous other early childhood intervention programs have been developed and offered in response to the strong evidence on the importance of SEL. A selection of these programs is listed in Table 3.3 (Alexander, 2018; Oh, 2018). The common features of these programs are that they provide a resource for teachers for implementation over a number of weeks or sessions. They share common objectives but have reported a range of different outcomes (Gershon & Pellitteri, 2018).

Unlike KidsMatter, which attempts to engage schools to focus on a comprehensive approach to social emotional aspects of education that incorporates parents, teachers and students in SEL aspects of the educational experience, the programs offer modules of instruction that can be incorporated into a pre-school environment over numerous sessions.

The Early Years Learning Framework for Australia *Belonging, Being and Becoming* (EYLF) (DEEWR, 2009) systematically addresses the learning outcomes that are consistent with those identified in Tables 3.1 and 3.2.

Key outcomes such as those in the *Belonging, Being and Becoming* document, are namely children:

- having a strong sense of identity
- being connected and contributing to their world
- having a strong sense of well-being
- being confident and involved learners
- being effective communicators.

Table 3.3 SEL programs in a pre-school setting[5]

SEL Program	Implementation	Targeted Competencies	Competencies Measured
Strong Start Pre-K (Gunter, Caldarella, Korth & Young, 2012) – USA	Participant: Pre-K children Facilitator: Teacher Structure: 10 lessons with 2 optional booster sessions Frequency and Duration: 2 lessons a week over 6-week period	Internalising problem behaviours, vocabulary to express feelings	Teacher reported emotional regulation, internalising behaviour, student–teacher relationship
Social-Emotional Prevention Program (SEP) (Stefan, 2012) – Romania	Participant: High risk Pre-school children Facilitator: Teacher Structure: 5 modules embedded in class activities, includes teacher and parent training Frequency and Duration: 5 modules over 5-month period	Emotional competencies (e.g. emotion knowledge and regulation), social competencies (e.g. compliance to rules, problem-solving, prosocial behaviours, cooperation)	Teacher reported social competence (e.g. joyful, secure, tolerant, integrated, calm, prosocial, cooperative, autonomous), externalising and internalising problems Parent reported social skills (e.g. cooperation, assertion, responsibility, self-control), externalising problems Children assessment of emotion knowledge, social problem-solving skills
Second Step Early Learning (SSEL) (Upshur, Heyman & Wenz-Gross, 2017) – USA	Participant: 3–5 years old Facilitator: Trained teacher Structure: 5 units Frequency and Duration: 28 weekly themes with different activities, brain builder and songs for 5 days of the week	Skills for learning, empathy, emotion management, friendship skills and problem-solving, transition to kindergarten	Child assessment of emotional knowledge, prosocial behaviour, executive function

Program	Participants / Facilitator / Structure / Duration	Content / Skills	Outcomes
Animal Fun (Piek et al., 2013) – Australia	Participants: Pre-school children (4–6 years old) Facilitator: Trained Teacher Structure: 9 modules (4 modules and gross motor, 4 modules on fine motor and 1 module on social emotional) Duration and Frequency: 30 mins a day, 4 days per week, minimum of 10 weeks	Gross motor development, fine motor development, social emotional skills (e.g. laughter, relaxation, emotions)	Teacher reported motor proficiency, hyperactivity, emotional symptoms, conduct problems, peer relationship, prosocial behaviour
Pre-school Promoting Alternative Thinking Strategies (PATHS) (Hamre, Pianta, Mashburn & Downer, 2012) – USA	Participants: Pre-school children (4 years old) Facilitator: Trained teacher Structure: 36 lessons, organised into 8 units, delivered during circle time Duration and Frequency: 15–30 mins, minimum once per week	Prosocial friendship skills, emotion understanding and expression skills, self-control, problem-solving (interpersonal negotiation and conflict resolution)	Teacher reported social competence, social problems
Social-Emotional Learning Facilitator (SELF KIT) (Opre & Buzgar, 2012) – Romania	Participants: Pre-school children (4–6 years old) Facilitator: Trained Teacher Structure: 8 modules Duration and Frequency: 1 module per week	Rational emotive behavioural therapy principles, irrational beliefs, relationship between cognitive and emotion, change unhealthy thoughts	Parent, teacher and psychologist reported social competencies, emotional competencies, cognitive competencies, motor competencies, personal autonomy, disruptive behaviour, anxiety
Connecting with Others (Schultz, Richardson, Barber & Wilcox, 2011) – USA	Participants: Low income, at-risk pre-school children (3–5 years old) Facilitator: Teachers Structure: 30 lessons divided into 6 skill areas Duration and Frequency: Hour long lesson, 1–2 lessons per week	Concept of self and others, socialisation, problem-solving/conflict resolution, communication, sharing, empathy/caring	Teacher reported problematic behaviours, emotional problems, attention problems, atypicality, withdrawal, adaptability, social skills, leadership, functional communication

(Continued)

Table 3.3 (Cont.)

SEL Program	Implementation	Targeted Competencies	Competencies Measured
Social-emotional program for kindergarten (Adela, Mihaela, Elena-Adriana & Monica, 2011) – Romania	Participants: 3-7 years old Facilitator: Trained teacher Structure: Implement strategies and curricula activities learned Duration and Frequency: Daily interaction in a month – 30-week program	Social emotional competence, behavioural competence	Teacher and parent reported emotional competence (e.g. emotion understanding, expression and self-regulation), social competence (e.g. rile compliance, social interaction, prosocial behaviour)
Pre-school RULER Yale Centre for Emotional Intelligence (2018) USA	Participant: Pre-school children aged 3-5 Facilitator: Trained adults in children's life Structure: School-wide; Whole classroom; Teacher training in emotional skills. Frequency and Duration: SEL is embedded throughout each pre-school day.	Emotional intelligence and emotional literacy	Using the mood meter and tests of emotional labeling and recognition to assess children's social emotional skills. Higher scores in intervention group (Rivers, et.al., 2015).
Zippy's Friends Partnership for Children, (2018a, b). UK	Participant: 5-7 year olds Also adapted for special needs children, and autism Facilitator: Trained teachers Frequency and Duration: 24 week	Based on Folkman & Lazarus model of stress and coping (1984). Also teaches recognising feelings, self-control and assertiveness (Mishara & Ystgaard, 2006)	More positive coping, improved social skills (i.e. cooperation, assertion and self-control. Teachers report self-awareness and emotional recognition (Lawson, Stenfert, Kroese, & Unwin (2015).
COPE-R (ELC, 2019) AUSTRALIA	Participant: 3-6 year olds Facilitator: Teacher Structure: 6 modules Frequency and Duration: six modules can be embedded in daily teaching or run as sessions over a six-week period.	Caring for others, open communication, politeness and empathic sharing. Use modalities such as art, dance, discussion and role play.	Higher teachers rated positive coping and prosocial behaviour compared to control group (Cornell et al., 2017; Pang, Frydenberg, Liang & Deans, 2018).

5 Acknowledgements to Monique Alexander and Boon Chin Oh (2018) for their compilation of SEL programs in pre-school settings.

Each of these outcomes are elaborated in the form of competencies in the context of early childhood education. Early childhood pedagogy takes account of partnerships, particularly those between parents and teachers and indeed cross-generationally such as that detailed in Chapter 9 describing an intergenerational program in an early learning setting. Pedagogy incorporates a respect for diversity, high expectations and equity as defining elements of good educational practice. Additionally, classroom practice involves holistic approaches to children, learning through play both intentionally and through informal learning activities. The learning outcomes are extensively detailed as to how they are evident and how to promote. In many of the programs that are listed in Table 3.3 similar goals and outcomes are achieved through various activities such as movement, role play and classroom discussion (see Chapter 8 for an illustration of the implementation of one of the SEL programs in a pre-school setting, namely, COPE-Resilience).

Take home messages

- The benefits of SEL in education are now well established.
- Policies and guidelines across international communities are quite consistent.
- Applications in educational practice vary from policy injunctions, to the development of practices across the whole school community and the application of particular programs for early childhood settings.
- SEL programs build competencies in the early childhood years.

References

Adela, M., Mihaela, S., Elena-Adriana, T., & Monica, F. (2011). Evaluation of a program for developing socio-emotional competencies in pre-school children. *Social and Behavioral Sciences*, *30*, 2161–2164.

Alexander, M. (2018). *Social and emotional learning: The building blocks of pre-school mental health and coping*. (Unpublished master thesis). University of Melbourne, Melbourne, Australia.

Allison, C., Baron-Cohen, S., Wheelwright, S., Stone, M., & Muncer, S. (2011). Psychometric analysis of the empathy quotient (EQ). *Personality and Individual Differences*, *51*(7), 829–835. doi:10.1016/j.paid.2011.07.005

Australian Children's Education & Care Quality Authority. (2018). *Guide to the national quality framework*. Retrieved 2 April 2019 from https://www.acecqa.gov.au/sites/default/files/2019-07/Guide-to-the-NQF.pdf

Australian Curriculum, Assessment and Reporting Authority (ACARA). (2012). *General capabilities*. Retrieved from www.australiancurriculum.edu.au/generalcapabilities/personal-and-social-capability/introduction/introduction

Bailey, C. S., Rivers, S. E.,Tominey, S. L., O'Bryon, E. C., Olsen, S. G., Sneeden, C. K., Peisch, V. D., Gal, D. E., & Brackett, M. A. (2019). *Promoting early childhood social and emotional learning with Preschool RULER.* New Haven, CT, USA: Manuscript submitted for publication, Yale Child Study Center, Yale School of Medicine.

Baron-Cohen, S., & Wheelwright, S. (2004). The empathy quotient: An investigation of adults with Asperger syndrome or high functioning autism, and normal sex differences. *Journal of Autism and Developmental Disorders, 34*(2), 163–175.

Bertram, T., & Pascal, C. (2016). *Early childhood policies and systems in eight countries: Findings from IEA's early childhood education study.* Springer International Publishing. Retrieved from www.iea.nl/fileadmin/user_upload/Publications/Electronic_versions/ECES-policies_and_systems-report.pdf

Bierman, K. L., & Motamedi, M. (2015). Social-emotional learning programs for preschool children. In E. Frydenberg, A. Martin, & R. Collie (Eds.), *Handbook of social and emotional learning: Research and practice* (pp. 135–151.). Singapore: Springer.

Blair, C., & Raver, C. C. (2016). Poverty, stress, and brain development: New directions for prevention and intervention. *Academic Pediatrics, 16*(3), S30–S36. doi:10.1016/j.acap.2016.01.010

Bull, R., Espy, K. A., & Wiebe, S. (2008). Short term memory, working memory, and executive functioning in pre-schoolers: Longitudinal predictors of mathematical achievement at 7 years. *Developmental Neuropsychology, 33,* 205–228.

Burdelski, M. (2010). Socializing politeness routines: Action, other-orientation, and embodiment in a Japanese pre-school. *Journal of Pragmatics, 42*(6), 1606–1621. doi:10.1016/j.pragma.2009.11.007

Carreras, M. R., Braza, P., Muñoz, J. M., Braza, F., Azurmendi, A., Pascual-Sagastizabal, E., ... Sánchez-Martín, J. R. (2014). Aggression and prosocial behaviours in social conflicts mediating the influence of cold social intelligence and affective empathy on children's social preference. *Scandinavian Journal of Psychology, 55*(4), 371–379. doi:10.1111/sjop.12126

Caselman, T. (2007). *Teaching children empathy, the social emotion: Lessons, activities and reproducible worksheets (K-6) that teach how to 'step into other's shoes'.* Chapin, SC: YouthLight Incorporated.

Cicchetti, D., & Blender, J. A. (2006). A multiple-levels-of-analysis perspective on resilience: Implications for the developing brain, neural plasticity, and preventive interventions. *Annals of the New York Academy of Sciences, 1094,* 248–258. doi:10.1196/annals.1376.029

Collaborative for Academic, Social and Emotional Learning (CASEL). (2013). *Social and emotional learning core competencies.* Retrieved from: www.casel.org/social-and-emotional-learning/core-competencies.

Commonwealth of Australia. (2009). *Belonging, Being and Becoming: An Early Years Learning Framework for Australia.* Canberra: Australian Government.

Cornell, C., Kiernan, N., Kaufman, D., Dobee, P., Frydenberg, E., & Deans, J. (2017). Developing social emotional competence in the early years. In E. Frydenberg, A. J. Martin, & R. J. Collie (Eds.), *Social and emotional learning in Australia and the Asia-Pacific* (pp. 391–441). Singapore: Springer.

Dachyshyn, D. M. (2015). Being mindful, heartful, and ecological in early years care and education. *Contemporary Issues in Early Childhood, 16*(1), 32–41. doi:10.1177/1463949114566756

Decety, J. (2011). The neuroevolution of empathy. *Annals of the New York Academy of Sciences, 1231,* 35–45.

Decety, J., Bartal, I. B., Uzefovsky, F., & Knafo-noam, A. (2015). Empathy as a driver of prosocial behaviour: Highly conserved neurobehavioural mechanisms across species. *Journal of Philosophical Transactions of the Royal Society B: Biological Sciences*, *371*, 1686.

DeMeulenaere, M. (2015). Promoting social and emotional learning in pre-school. *Dimensions of Early Childhood*, *43*(1), 8–10.

Denham, S., Bassett, H., & Zinsser, K. (2012). Early childhood teachers as socializers of young children's emotional competence. *Early Childhood Education Journal*, *40*(3), 137–143.

Department for Children, Schools and Families. (2007). *SEAL: Social and emotional aspects of learning for secondary schools: Tools for monitoring, profiling and evaluation.* Nottingham: DCSF Publications.

Department of Education, Employment and Workplace Relations for the Council of Australian Governments (DEEWR). (2009). *Belonging, being and becoming: The early years learning framework for Australia.* Canberra: Australian Government.

Department of Education, UK. (2017). *Early years foundation stage statutory framework (EYFS).* Retrieved from https://assets.publishing.service.gov.uk/government/uploads/system/uploads/attachment_data/file/596629/EYFS_STATUTORY_FRAMEWORK_2017.pdf

Diamond, A. (2002). Normal development of prefrontal cortex from birth to young adulthood: Cognitive functions, anatomy and biochemistry. In D. Stuss & R. Knight (Eds.), *Principles of frontal lobe function* (pp. 466–503). New York: Oxford University Press.

Durlak, J. A., Weissberg, R. P., Dymnicki, A. B., Taylor, R. D., & Schellinger, K. B. (2011). The impact of enhancing students' social and emotional learning: A meta-analysis of school-based universal interventions. *Child Development*, *82*(1), 405–432. doi:10.1111/j.1467-8624.2010.01564.x

Early Learning Centre. (2019). *COPE-R program.* Victoria: University of Melbourne.

Education Review Office (ERO). (2011). *Positive foundations for learning: Confident and competent children in early childhood services.* Retrieved 2 April 2019 fromhttps://www.ero.govt.nz/assets/Uploads/Positive-Foundations-for-Learning.pdf

Eisenberg, N., Cumberland, A., & Spinrad, T. L. (1998). Parental socialization of emotion. *Psychological Inquiry*, *9*(4), 241–273.

Elliott, S. N., Frey, J. R., & Davies, M. (2015). Systems for assessing and improving student's social skills to achieve academic competence. In J. A. Durlak, C. E. Domitrovich, R. P. Weissberg, & T. P. Gullotta (Eds.), *Handbook of social and emotional learning: Research and practice* (pp. 301–319). Guilford: New York.

Feshbach, N. D., & Feshbach, S. (2009). Empathy and education. In J. Decety & W. Ickes (Eds.), *The social neuroscience of empathy* (pp. 85–98). Cambridge, MA: The MIT Press.

Flook, L., Goldberg, S. B., Pinger, L., & Davidson, R. J. (2015). Promoting prosocial behavior and self-regulatory skills in pre-school children through a mindfulness-based kindness curriculum. *Developmental Psychology*, *51*(1), 44–51.

Fox, S., Levitt, P., & Nelson, C. (2010). How the timing and quality of early experiences influence the development of brain architecture. *Child Development*, *81*(1), 28–40. doi:10.1111/j.1467-8624.2009.01380.x

Frydenberg, E., & Deans, J. (2011). *The Early Years Coping Cards.* Melbourne, Vic.: ACER Press.

Frydenberg, E., Deans, J., & Liang, R. (2014). Families can do coping: Parenting skills in the early years. *Children Australia, 39*(2), 99–106.

Gershon, P., & Pellitteri, J. (2018). Promoting emotional intelligence in pre-school education: A review of programs. *International Journal of Emotional Education, 10* (2), 26–41.

Goleman, D. (2005). *Emotional intelligence.* New York: Bantam Books.

Gunter, L., Caldarella, P., Korth, B. B., & Young, K. R. (2012). Promoting social and emotional learning in pre-school students: A study of "strong start Pre-K". *Early Childhood Education Journal, 40*(3), 151–159.

Halberstadt, A. G., Denham, S. A., & Dunsmore, J. C. (2001). Affective social competence. *Social Development, 10*(1), 79–119. doi:10.1111/1467-9507.00150

Hamre, B. K., Pianta, R. C., Mashburn, A. J., & Downer, J. T. (2012). Promoting young children's social competence through the pre-school PATHS curriculum and MyTeachingPartner professional development resources. *Early Education & Development, 23*(6), 809–832. Retrieved from www.acecqa.gov.au/sites/default/files/2018-11/Guide-to-the-NQF_0.pdf. www.ero.govt.nz/publications/positive-foundations-for-learning-confident-and-competent-children-in-early-childhood-services/.

KidsMatter. (2016). *Resources for schools.* [online]. Retrieved 15 May 2016 from www.kidsmatter.edu.au/primary/resources-schools

KidsMatter Australia (2012). KidsMatter early childhood introduction. Retrieved 15 May 2016 from www.youtube.com/watch?v=HgyS-SV0Xyg

Lawson, A., Stenfert Kroese, B., & Unwin, G. (2015). *An independent evaluation of Zippy's Friends for children and young people with special educational needs.* Birmingham: University of Birmingham.

Lazarus, R. S., & Folkman, S. (1984). Coping. *Encyclopedia of Psychology, 1*, 294–296.

Lipton, M., & Nowicki, S. (2009). The Social Emotional Learning Framework (SELF): A guide for understanding brain-based Social Emotional Learning impairments. *The Journal of Developmental Processes, 4*, 99–115. doi:10.1037/a0033435

Littlefield, L., Cavanagh, S., Knapp, R., & O'Grady, L. (2017). KidsMatter: Building the capacity of Australian primary schools and early childhood services to foster children's social and emotional skills and promote children's mental health. In E. Frydenberg, A. Martin, & R. Collie (Eds.), *Social and emotional learning in Australia and the Asia-Pacific* (pp. 293–311). Singapore: Springer.

Macklem, G. L. (2008). *Practitioner's guide to emotion regulation in school-aged children.* New York: Springer. doi:10.1007/978-0-387-73851-2

McKown, C. (2015). Challenges and opportunities in the direct assessment of children's social-emotional comprehension. In J. A. Durlak, C. E. Domitrovich, R. P. Weissberg, & T. P. Gullotta (Eds.), *Handbook of social and emotional learning: Research and practice* (pp. 320–335). New York: Guilford.

Mishara, B. L., & Ystgaard, M. (2006). Effectiveness of a mental health promotion program to improve coping skills in young children: Zippy's Friends. *Early Childhood Research Quarterly, 21*(1), 110–123. doi:10.1016/j.ecresq.2006.01.002

Miyamoto, K., Huerta, M. C., & Kubacka, K. (2015). Fostering social and emotional skills for well-being and social progress. *European Journal of Education, 50* (2), 147–159.

Mortari, L. (2011). Thinking silently in the woods: Listening to children speaking about emotion. *European Early Childhood Education Research Journal, 19*(3), 345–356. doi:10.1080/1350293X.2011.597966

Myers, D. G. (2000). The funds, friends, and faith of happy people. *American Psychologist, 55*(1), 56–67.

O'Shea, M. (2005). *The brain: A very short introduction.* Oxford University Press. Retrieved from https://search-ebscohost-com.ezp.lib.unimelb.edu.au/login.aspx?direct=true&db=cat00006a&AN=melb.b5757394&site=eds-live&scope=site

Oh, B. C. (2018). *The impact of a Social Emotional Learning Program on pre-schoolers' social-emotional competence.* (Unpublished master thesis). University of Melbourne, Melbourne, Australia.

Opre, A., & Buzgar, R. (2012). The efficacy of SELF KIT program in developing socioemotional competencies of kindergarten children. *Social and Behavioral Sciences, 33,* 964–968.

Pang, D., Frydenberg, E., Liang, R., & Deans, J. (2018). Improving coping skills & promoting social and emotional competence in pre-schoolers: A 5-week COPE-R program. *Journal of Early Childhood Education Research, 7*(2), 1–31.

Partnerships for Children. (2018a). Teaching Zippy's Friends. Retrieved 22 September 2018, from www.partnershipforchildren.org.uk/teachers/zippy-s-friendsteachers/teaching-zippy-s-friends.html

Partnerships for Children. (2018b). Zippy's Friends. Retrieved 15 May 2018, from www.partnershipforchildren.org.uk/zippy-s-friends.html

Pianta, R., La Paro, K., & Hamre, B. K. (2008). *Classroom assessment scoring system (CLASS).* Baltimore, MD: Paul H. Brookes Publishing.

Piek, J. P., McLaren, S., Kane, R., Jensen, L., Dender, A., Roberts, C., … Straker, L. (2013). Does the Animal Fun program improve motor performance in children aged 4–6 years? *Human Movement Science, 32*(5), 1086–1096.

Rafaila, E. (2015). The competent teacher for teaching emotional intelligence. *Procedia - Social and Behavioral Sciences, 180,* 953–957. doi:10.1016/j.sbspro.2015.02.253

Rogoff, B. (1994). Developing understanding of the idea of communities of learners. *Mind, Culture, and Activity, 1*(4), 209–229.

Rosenthal, M., & Gatt, L. (2010). 'Learning to live together': Training early childhood educators to promote socio-emotional competence of toddlers and pre-school children. *European Early Childhood Education Research Journal, 18*(3), 223–240.

Schaps, E., & Battistich, V. (1991). Promoting health development through school-based prevention: New approaches. In E. Goplerude (Ed.), *Preventing adolescent drug use: From theory to practice, OSAP prevention monograph no. 8* (pp. 127–181). Washington, D.C.: U.S. Department of Health and Human Services.

Schultz, B. L., Richardson, R. C., Barber, C. R., & Wilcox, D. (2011). A pre-school pilot study of connecting with others: Lessons for teaching social and emotional competence. *Early Childhood Education Journal, 39*(2), 143–148.

Schwenck, C., Göhle, B., Hauf, J., Warnke, A., Freitag, C. M., & Schneider, W. (2014). Cognitive and emotional empathy in typically developing children: The influence of age, gender, and intelligence. *European Journal of Developmental Psychology, 11*(1), 63–76. doi:10.1080/17405629.2013.808994

Slee, P. T., Murray-Harvey, R., Dix, K. L., Skrzypiec, G., Askell-Williams, H., Lawson, M., & Krieg, S. (2012). *KidsMatter Early Childhood evaluation report*. Adelaide: Shannon Research Press.

Smith, C. A. (2013). Beyond 'I'm sorry': The educator's role in pre-schoolers' emergence of conscience. *YC: Young Children, 68*(1), 76–82.

Stefan, C. A. (2012). Social-emotional prevention program for pre-school children: An analysis of a high risk sample. *Cognition, Brain, Behavior, 16*(3), 319–356.

Thompson, R. A., Goodvin, R., & Meyer, S. (2006). Social development: Psychological understanding, self-understanding, and relationships. In J. L. Luby (Ed.), *Handbook of pre-school mental health: Development, disorders, and treatment* (pp. 3–22). New York, NY, US: The Guilford Press.

Upshur, C. C., Heyman, M., & Wenz-Gross, M. (2017). Efficacy trial of the Second Step Early Learning (SSEL) curriculum: Preliminary outcomes. Grantee Submission. Retrieved from https://ezp.lib.unimelb.edu.au/login?url=https://search.ebscohost.com/login.aspx?direct=true&db=eric&AN=ED573440&site=eds-live&scope=site

Waters, L., & White, M. (2015). Case study of a school wellbeing initiative: Using appreciative inquiry to support positive change. *International Journal of Wellbeing, 5*(1), 19–32.

Weare, K., & Gray, G. (2003). *What works in developing children's emotional and social competence and wellbeing?* (p. 113). London, UK: Department for Education and Skills.

Yale Centre for Emotional Intelligence. (2018). *Pre-school RULER: The mood meter in early childhood classrooms*. Retrieved 22 September 2018, from http://ei.yale.edu/pre-school-ruler/

Chapter 4

Early years visual coping tools

Operationalising social and emotional competencies in pre-school children

'When someone says that they don't like you, you become so sad that you want to hide away.'

~ Paige, 4-year-old

'When people are kind to you, you are kind to them.'

~ Zac, 5-year-old

Overview

This chapter provides an opportunity for readers to gain a deeper insight into children's capacity to articulate their thoughts, feelings and actions about how they manage everyday challenging situations. It offers detailed examples of how visual images may be used by adults to engage young children in discussions about coping and coping-related activities in both the educational and family context. This includes a focus on how adults can cultivate a safe and secure space to effectively engage their children in deeper meaningful conversations. Children are provided with building blocks with which to develop social and emotional competence through learning to share understandings as an outcome of conversations with adults. The cards provide a stimulus and a 'way in' through images representing stressful situations and coping options.

Development of the Early Years Coping Cards

There has been a growing emphasis on the importance of Social Emotional Learning in children from the outset of their lives. From infancy onwards, the attachment relationships and skills learned in the family and child related settings are what buttresses children's lived experiences and builds the skills that they need to achieve their milestones and traverse their pre-school, school and post-school years successfully. Given that well-being and resilience are important goals, what are the coping resources that children need to achieve these desired outcomes?

Background research on early years coping

It is readily agreed that social emotional competence is an asset both in the pre-school years and beyond. Denham (2006) cited extensive research which could be summed up as indicating that young children who enter school with more 'positive profiles' of social emotional competence have more positive attitudes about school and have better early adjustments along with improved grades. Conversely, deficits in those areas puts young children at risk of experiencing multiple problems including victimisation and less success.

Children, like adolescents and adults, experience emotions that they utilise to deal with everyday life. Similarly, children, like adolescents and adults, see situations as one of stress, loss, harm or challenge with which they have to deal; that is coping.

The early researchers in the field of coping in young children summarised the field in several reviews. The first was by Fields & Prinz (1997) who considered eight studies and found that much of the research to date had focused on medical procedures and academic stressors. Four of the eight studies focused on social stressors with more problem-solving strategies being used than emotion-focused ones. When five of the studies compared the coping strategies of 3–7-year-olds with those of older children aged 8–12 they found that problem-solving strategies use declined and there was an increased use of emotion-focused strategies. The second of these reviews by Compas, Connor-Smith, Saltzman, Thomsen & Wadsworth (2001) reviewed 60 studies where they did not find a consensus among the coping dimensions that were used across the studies. Nevertheless, we know that young children have concerns or worries with which they have to deal, and whilst there isn't universal agreement on descriptors of coping strategies used, there are likely to be a greater range of emotions vented as children grow beyond the early years.

From early years research since 2010 we know that, in general, the concerns of 3–6-year-olds can be summarised as feelings of uncertainty in new situations, fear of abandonment by a significant adult, fear of sadness about rejection or not having a friend, fear of losing control such as wetting oneself or fear of being reprimanded or punished by parents or teachers.

Operationalising early years coping

A multiphase program of early years research, much of it in the classroom with children as key informants, was validated with data derived from parents. The program of research aimed to establish clarity around the concepts and constructs that children in the early years use both to describe and understand their coping in context and also to then be able to utilise these strategies to develop helpful coping skills. Phase One of the project established the situations that concern 4-year-olds along with the constructs and concepts that relate to how they cope. That is, how children articulate their thoughts, feelings and actions when challenged by their concerns. It was found that parents reported that their children used fewer coping strategies with a larger number of passive strategies used than did teachers or children (Deans, Frydenberg & Tsurutani, 2010). Having done that, the researchers developed a set of visual tools, the Early Years Coping Cards, that depict a range of visual representations of challenging situations that can be used to stimulate children's verbal responses to describe their coping strategies (Frydenberg & Deans, 2011).

The visual tools are used as exemplars of the concepts and constructs that educators and those working with children may choose to use. Alternately professionals may choose to develop their own visual images to engage in conversations around situations and consider how to deal with the challenges of everyday life.

There are seven age-appropriate challenging situations using visual images to capture the full range of coping strategies described by pre-schoolers and the frequency of use of the different coping strategies across the situations. The situations that were included were 1) separation from a parent, 2) friendship, 3) don't like something, 4) being reprimanded by a teacher, 5) teasing, 6) night fears and 7) making a choice. The methodology is detailed in Chalmers, Frydenberg & Deans (2011). The children were asked whether they would like to talk to the interviewers and, following consent, the children were then asked, 'What do you see in this picture?', 'Has this ever happened to you?', and if yes, 'How did you feel when this happened to you?', and if no, 'How do you think the child in the picture feels?'. If the child showed a negative emotion the child would be asked 'What would you do to make yourself feel better?' and/or 'What would you say to the person to make themselves feel better?'. The responses were collated and coded and compared to earlier studies (Deans et al., 2010) to form a total of 15 potential coping strategies, namely, Play/do something else, Work to solve the problem, Do nothing/don't know what to do, Seek comfort, Think positive, Cry/can't feel better, Ignore the problem, Seek help, Complain of illness, Blame others, Calm down, Tantrums, Talk about it, Keep feelings to self and/or get angry with self. The coping strategies were grouped into productive and non-productive or less helpful ones (Table 4.1).

From the data provided by the children and that complemented by focus groups conducted with the parents, the images were developed to reflect children's coping using the situation images as prompts. Additionally, there were over 268 different coping strategies articulated by the 46 4-year-olds and these were grouped into 40 strategies which in turn could be grouped further to capture these young people's coping to become the visual representations of coping in the Early Years Coping Cards (Figure 4.1).

Application of the Early Years Coping Cards

The Early Years Coping Cards were developed to be used in multiple settings such as in early childhood centres and homes with teachers and parents (Deans,

Table 4.1 Productive and non-productive coping strategies reported by pre-schoolers

Productive Coping	Non-Productive Coping
Seek comfort*	Seek comfort*
Play/do something else	Do nothing/don't know
Solve the problem	Cry/can't feel better
Think positive/calm down	Get angry/tantrum
Ignore problem	Keep feelings to self
	Complain of illness
	Blame others
Seek help	
Talk about it	

*Seek comfort was reported by children in this study for both productive and non-productive coping. That is, sometimes it is helpful and at other times not. For example, it might be a way of calming oneself or a way of avoiding dealing with the problem.

Figure 4.1 Early Years Coping Cards[1]

---

1 The Early Years Coping Cards are colourful. They are published by Australian Council for Educational Research (ACER) and available for purchase at their website: www.acer.org. Alternately, it is possible to utilise the concepts and represent them in any desired visual medium such as cartoons, collages, line drawings etc. Importantly the images should be engaging for the age group in a particular context with which they are to be utilised.

Frydenberg & Liang, 2012). Whilst the situations that are experienced by parents or teachers may be different to those experienced by children, the language of coping has been kept closely similar when developing teaching resources and measurement tools (see Chapter 5). The images described in this chapter can be used to encourage conversations about challenging situations, and how to manage both the situation and the emotions that occur as a result of it. The visual tools help parents, teachers, clinicians or others working with young children to focus on everyday challenging situations that may cause uncertainty or fear. They have been designed to facilitate learning outcomes including:

- How to respect self and others
- Relationships and the importance of friendship
- How to communicate feelings appropriately
- Who they are and their place in the world
- Cultural diversity and difference
- Empathy and care for others and the environment.

The images represent the situations that are of concern to children and coping concepts that they utilise. Once the concepts are identified they can be visually represented in any graphic form and used in similar ways to what is described in this volume. The images help to create an opportunity to begin a conversation with a child or group of children as a social emotional tool which can be used in any context be it home, early years setting or clinic.

Using the cards in different context

Children (4–7 years of age) are not only competent thinkers and communicators about their own emotions and the emotions of others, but they also have the capacity for deep reflection and develop complex arguments around emotions when given the conversational prompts (Mortari, 2011). Frydenberg, Deans & Liang (2014) demonstrated that children can learn helpful coping skills through modelling by adults, and interactions between adults and children. In the educational context this can be achieved through direct teaching, through interactive play with the cards or through role-plays and games that identify issues of concern and how children can deal with their worries (see Chapter 8). Below are examples of how the Early Years Coping Cards are utilised in a pre-school setting by teachers using the see-think-feel-do questions as prompters (see Table 4.2, Table 4.3, Table 4.4 and Table 4.5 as examples).
Example 1: Teasing (Figure 4.2)
Example 2: Separation from parent (Figure 4.3)
Example 3: Friendship (Figure 4.4)
Example 4: Making a choice (Figure 4.5)

Figure 4.2 Situation card: teasing

Table 4.2 Teacher facilitating a group discussion with the teasing card

Teacher Instruction	Children's Responses
What do you see?	'Somebody teasing another person.' 'A big kid teasing a little kid because he has a tory bunny rabbit.' 'I think the little kid had the rabbit first but the other kid snatched if off them.' 'Maybe the big guy doesn't like pink and the little guy does and he's teasing him.' 'I think he's teasing. I think the big kid wants it 'cause the little kid wants it.'
What do you think?	'He must have gone into his room at night and taken it.' 'The little kid was being naughty, and the grown-up took it off him.' 'I think the little boy was playing at first, then the big kid took it away.' 'I think the little kid was playing with it and the big kid came and took it off him and said, "If you don't give me that, you're not coming to my party".'
What do you feel?	Bad, sad, angry, upset, crying, disappointment, frustrated, nervous, not good, worried.
What do you do?	'I would say "don't do it".' 'I would say "I don't like it and stop it now".' 'Please stop it and walk away.' 'I would walk away and tell the teacher.' 'Tell my mum and dad.' 'I would walk away and if I was at school, I would tell the teachers.'

(Continued)

Table 4.2 (Cont).

Teacher Instruction	Children's Responses

Teachers' creative approach: See and tell
The teacher held the large situation[2] card to the group and allowed children to discuss what they thought was happening, why, and what they would do in this situation. The teacher reflected that she found using the smaller cards in a large group worked well, as she asked the children to choose a card that interested them (a situation they have been in before) and then asked them to explain what was happening in the picture, have they ever been in this situation and how have they coped with it. It was helpful for children who have been in the situation but didn't have any suggestions on how they have coped with it, as other children were able to share with that child how they have coped and suggest a range of strategies they could try. The teacher thought that it worked well, allowing the children to see that they are not alone in what they feel in different situations and that many of us deal with similar problems or anxieties and that it's okay.

Bringing creativity to build the shared language of coping

There are an infinite range of situations that children find themselves in and likewise an infinite range of coping strategies that can be called upon. The range of situations and coping strategies are often determined by the context and the person using the cards is encouraged to augment the list by what is considered appropriate to meet the needs of individuals or groups of children. Therefore, two blank cards can be used for such situations. A parent or educator may also use the blank card to discuss anything else or have a thinking space or breathing space with their children. Alternatively, images can be cut out from magazines or downloaded from the internet as required to create a collection of cards that meet particular requirements.

This chapter highlights the benefits of building a shared language of coping between children, parents and teachers in order to effectively engage children in deeper and more meaningful conversations around coping, thereby contributing to healthy adaptation to everyday experiences in the early years. Having developed the visual tools around coping in the early years subsequent phases of the research program explored ways to measure coping which are described in Chapter 5. The relationship between anxiety and coping has been explored in numerous ways (Pang, Frydenberg & Deans, 2015; Yeo, Frydenberg, Northam & Deans, 2014) and is described in Chapter 6, and families' approaches to coping is considered in Chapter 7.

---

2 Situation cards were larger (e.g. A5) than the coping cards.

Figure 4.3 Situation card: saying goodbye to parent

Table 4.3 Teacher facilitating a group discussion with the saying goodbye to parent card

Teacher Instruction	Children's Responses
What do you see?	'The boy is going to school and the boy is waving goodbye.' 'The mummy is dropping the children at school and saying goodbye.' 'The boy is saying goodbye to mummy at kinder.'
What do you think?	'I think the little boy is a bit worried that his mummy is not coming with him.' 'I think he is sad because he doesn't know where to go.' 'Maybe he is sad because he doesn't know anyone at kinder.' 'I think he is sad to say goodbye to mummy. He wants to stay with mummy.'
What do you feel?	'I'm sad when I come to kinder sometimes, not because I don't like to come to kinder, I just want to stay with mum and dad.' 'All I want is to go home with mummy. I'm sad.'
What do you do?	Cry and scream; hug a toy; play; talk to teacher. 'I will cry and cry until mummy comes back. I don't know what time mummy is coming back.'

Teachers' creative approach: Scatter and select
Teachers have placed the situation card and the coping cards on display in the room and have encouraged those children with separation difficulties to look at and talk about the coping cards with their parents at drop off in the morning and talked about what he/she is going to do after mum and dad has left. Teachers reported them as being very useful in that situation.

Figure 4.4 Situation card: friendship

Table 4.4 Teacher facilitating a group discussion with the friendship card

Teacher Instruction	Children's Responses
What do you see?	'These two children are not sharing with the other boy.' 'The two children are playing with the ball and not letting the other boy play.'
What do you think?	'They don't want to play with him because he is not their friend.' 'Maybe only two people are allowed to play in that game.' 'The boy asked "can I play with you?" but they didn't hear. I think the boy should turn around and speak louder.' 'I think they are ignoring them.'
What do you feel?	'It's not kind not to let other children play.' 'They are not sharing, and it is not nice.' 'Those children are not sharing and that makes the other boy really sad.'
What do you do?	'Go and play somewhere else.' 'Tell the teachers, maybe they can help.' 'Play by yourself for a while and find somewhere else to play again later.' 'He can play with his own toy.'

Teachers' creative approach: Display and discuss
The situation cards and the coping cards are all displayed in the room. Whenever there were situations related to 'friendship', the group refers to the coping cards. The teacher reported that it has helped greatly with the children, particularly those who always have difficulty in coping with a friendship-related situation.

Figure 4.5 Situation card: making a choice

Table 4.5 Teacher facilitating a group discussion with the making a choice card

Teacher Instruction	Children's Responses
What do you see?	'The little boy is thinking who to play with.' 'The boy is deciding whether to play with the ball or the tea set.' 'The boy is choosing to play with the boys or the girls.'
What do you think?	'I think he can't decide.' 'I think he might be choosing to play with the boys because he is a boy.' 'Boys can play with girls too. I play with girls.' 'Maybe the girls don't want to play with the boys.'
What do you feel?	'Sometimes I don't know who to play with.' 'Sometimes I want to play with some children, but they don't want to play with me.' 'I think he cannot decide, and he is a bit sad.'
What do you do?	'I will go and play with the boys first, then go and play with the girls.' 'Maybe they can all play together.' 'Sometimes you choose where your best friend is playing too. But friends don't have to play together all the time.'

Teachers' creative approach: Display and play
The group talked about what factors to consider in making a choice – making 'safe choices', 'wise choices' and 'kind choices'. This was a follow-up of the discussion they had about 'gentle hands', 'helpful hands' and 'wise hands'. The coping cards and situation card are displayed in the room for further discussion about making 'safe', 'wise' and 'kind' choices in response to children's recent 'unwise' choices and 'unsafe' choices made during play.

Take home messages

From extensive research in the field of coping and particularly with young children it was established that:

- Children can identify a range of coping strategies.
- Visual tools can be utilised to engage children with peers or adults in conversations relating to coping.
- Visual tools can be used to encourage children's use of helpful strategies and to reduce the use of the unhelpful ones.
- Boys and girls cope differently.
- Coping can be learned, and skills can be developed.
- There is no right or wrong coping, but the situation determines the best strategy to use.
- Coping strategies fall broadly into two categories, productive and non-productive (sometimes called helpful and less helpful).

References

Chalmers, K., Frydenberg, E., & Deans, J. (2011). An exploration into the coping strategies of pre-schoolers: Implications for professional practice. *Australian Academic Press, 36*(3), 120–127.

Compas, B. E., Connor-Smith, J. K., Saltzman, H., Thomsen, A. H., & Wadsworth, M. E. (2001). Coping with stress during childhood and adolescence: Problems, progress, and potential in theory and research. *Psychological Bulletin, 127*(1), 87–127.

Deans, J., Frydenberg, E., & Liang, R. (2012). Building a shared language of coping: Dynamics of communication between parents and pre-school children. *New Zealand Research into Early Childhood Research Journal, 15*, 67–89.

Deans, J., Frydenberg, E., & Tsurutani, H. (2010). Operationalising social and emotional coping competencies in kindergarten children. *New Zealand Research In Early Childhood Education, 13*, 113–124.

Denham, S. A. (2006). Social-emotional competence as support for school readiness: What is it and how do we assess it? *Early Education and Development, 17*(1), 57–89.

Fields, L., & Prinz, R. J. (1997). Coping and adjustment during childhood and adolescence. *Clinical Psychology Review, 17*(8), 937–976.

Frydenberg, E., & Deans, J. (2011). *Early Years Coping Cards: User guide.* Camberwell, Victoria: ACER Press.

Frydenberg, E., Deans, J., & Liang, R. (2014). Families can do coping: Parenting skills in the early years. *Children Australia, 39*(2), 99–106.

Mortari, L. (2011). Thinking silently in the woods: Listening to children speaking about emotion. *European Early Childhood Education Research Journal, 19*(3), 345–356. doi:10.1080/1350293X.2011.597966

Pang, I., Frydenberg, E., & Deans, J. (2015). The relationship between anxiety and coping in pre-schoolers. In P. Buchenwald & K. Moore (Eds.), *Anxiety, stress & coping* (pp. 26–27). Berlin: Verlag.

Yeo, K., Frydenberg, E., Northam, E., & Deans, J. (2014). Coping with stress among pre-school children and associations with anxiety level and controllability of situations. *Australian Journal of Psychology, 66*(2), 93–101. doi:10.1111/ajpy.12047

Chapter 5

Measuring coping in a pre-school population

'Your body is relaxed when you are happy.'

~ Mars, 4-year-old

'Your body is fast when you are playing with your friends.'

~ Henry, 4-year-old

'Tears can come from anger, you can even be angry with yourself.'

~ Lily, 4-year-old

'When the tears come you know that you are really, really sad.'

~ Oasis, 5-year-old

Overview

When it comes to measurement and evaluation, there is no 'one size fits all' approach. We can utilise tools, frameworks and best practice to develop and utilise the best measurement tools in the context at hand. Measurement may have a purpose that goes beyond data gathering and has applications that benefit a population. The benefits and pitfalls of measurement, particularly as it applies to children, are considered. We know from the previous chapters that it is possible to consider coping at an early age in that pre-schoolers are capable of articulating a wide range of coping strategies for different situations. Firstly, in this chapter, adult coping constructs are introduced as it is considered important that adults, be they teachers or parents, be familiar with coping language and consider their own coping prior to working with children in their charge. However, a growing body of research suggests that coping in young children does not align with the common adult taxonomies of problem-focused versus emotion-focused coping or active versus passive coping. This chapter will outline a body of research which has identified age-appropriate use of children's coping language and the development and validation of the Children's Coping Scale – Revised (CCS-R) to measure the coping construct in pre-school populations. Practical implications from the CCS-R study's findings are discussed for educators and parents to consider as tools to inform practice.

The paradox of measurement

There is a paradox when it comes to the measurement of a psychological construct like coping for the purposes of information gathering; it can be harmful when the information is used to categorise or label people. That is, there are both uses and abuses of measurement. The uses relate to information gathering that is helpful for understanding and the abuses relate to how information can be used to categorise or label a child. This is often done at an unconscious level where an adult or a peer may be perceived as 'a cry baby' or someone who is always 'so good'. The labels in themselves can become self-fulfilling prophecies as the child may feel that they have to live up to expectations, whether good or bad. In contrast, assessment may be used to facilitate understanding of what is occurring in a particular context which may not generalise to other settings. Assessment may draw attention to a child's specific needs and can helpfully influence the way a parent or teacher deals with a child in a particular setting.

How psychologists measure

The first step when psychologists want to develop measurement tools is to identify concepts and constructs to be measured. That in itself is a useful process, particularly when one is interested in a specific population or age group. The concepts and constructs have to be age- appropriate and socio-culturally relevant. When it comes to measuring coping, researchers have done that with all age groups, firstly with adults, then with adolescents and more recently with pre-school-aged children.

In order to develop measurement tools, researchers first identified situations that may be of concern to a population of interest (a group of adults or a group of 3- to 5-year-olds in the pre-school context) and then we asked them how they might deal with such situations. As we developed the Coping Scale for Adults (Frydenberg & Lewis, 1997; Frydenberg & Lewis, 2014) and subsequently the visual tools described in Chapter 4 we identified the following situations that were of concern to 3- and 4-year-olds: saying goodbye to a parent, fear of the dark, having to try something new, losing something such as a broken toy, having to choose between friends or feeling left out. Theoretically there are an infinite number of concerns, but these were the ones we identified as being most salient to our pre-school population. Whatever the context in which the questioning is done the situation has to be relevant to that population. We then invited children to describe how they cope with any of the relevant situations. Having developed thousands of age-appropriate and situation-appropriate coping thoughts, feelings and actions we were able to group them and validate that they accurately reflected the constructs. All that is fine if you want to use a coping tool or measure just to gather information that describes an individual or groups' adaptation and use it for teaching purposes. That was the motivation for developing the coping images. See Chapter 4 for the description and use of the Early Years Coping Cards (Frydenberg & Deans, 2011a).

However, researchers and practitioners want to go a lot further. Researchers want to understand how a particular population, such as 3-year-old girls or 5-year-old boys, for example, cope and how their coping is associated with well-being, self-regulation, empathy and so on, as well as trying to achieve an understanding of how the coping skills can be taught. That is the useful information that provides much of the data upon which this book is based. The problem arises when these measurement tools are considered to be 'hard-nosed' science, which leads people to categorise individuals or groups such as those who are good copers and those who are bad copers. That is fraught with danger as it may lead to labelling and consequently may lead to behaviours that are expected. Where, for example, the child develops a persona according to the descriptor that has been ascribed to him or her, this is often termed the self-fulfilling prophecy.

How one copes can change and does change across the lifespan. We are indeed in different situations throughout the lifespan so coping changes according to development, social learning through observing how others cope, through one's own experience and according to the situation. Children develop, and psychosocial development continues throughout childhood and into adulthood as circumstances come to play their part in shaping what a person does.

What we know about how adults cope

Coping has been conceptualised as thoughts, feelings and actions that arise in response to demands placed upon an individual. Some strategies attempt to remove or to remedy the source of the demand (e.g. problem-solving), others help individuals to accommodate to it (e.g. seek a relaxing diversion) and there are strategies that demonstrate an inability to deal with the demand (e.g. despair or get sick) (Frydenberg, 2018). The most frequently cited categorisation of coping actions has been into those that deal with a problem (problem-focused) and those that deal with emotions (emotion-focused) (Lazarus & Folkman, 1984). However, more recently it has been helpful to consider coping according to outcomes that are helpful and those that are not helpful, and these have been labelled *productive* and *non-productive*. The many ways to assess coping generally have in common a set of descriptions or single actions which are grouped into coping strategies where there is a similarity of concept or ideation. These in turn can be further grouped more broadly into commonality of practice. Coping instruments have been generally developed through self-reports, semi-structured interviews, daily diary recordings, observation of behaviour and the reports of significant others, such as parents, teachers and peers.

Development of adult coping measure

A 60-item instrument (CSA-2, Frydenberg & Lewis, 2014) has been developed to assess how adults cope. The tool can be used for self-assessment and reflection on whether a set of coping actions are helpful or unhelpful and whether the individual wants to change something the next time they meet the same situation. In a parent context it is also useful to acknowledge that people cope in different ways. For example, males and females generally cope differently, so in a parent context accepting differences between partners, between parents and children or between children, can be helpful. The 60 items of CSA-2 describe coping actions which in turn are grouped into 20 categories or subscales and into three styles of coping which are generally used by adults: productive coping style, nonproductive coping style and problem-solving coping style. Figure 5.1 identifies the groupings with a description of what they mean, thus providing a language of coping for parents and teachers.

Productive Coping	Non-Productive Coping	Problem-Solving
The productive coping style reflects an attempt to focus on the positive, seek spiritual help, attend to ones' self-image, retain a sense of humour and improve relationships, while finding time to relax and attempting to put the problem out of one's mind.	Non-productive coping, is characterised by a focus on the negative, worrying, blaming oneself, becoming physically unwell, and trying to relieve the stress by crying, screaming, drink or drugs, because these strategies relate negatively to desired outcomes.	A coping style that encompasses focusing on solving problems while maintaining a social dimension characterised by social action, seeking professional help and/or social support.

Figure 5.1 Three coping styles identified in adults (from CSA-2)

Coping with parenting

WHY IT MATTERS HOW PARENTS COPE

A body of research in adult coping has highlighted the impact that different coping styles have on an individual's well-being. The use of productive coping strategies is linked to higher self-esteem, higher internal locus of control, deeper learning and greater well-being. Conversely, the use of non-productive coping strategies is linked with the inverse of the above, with some of the poorest personal outcomes associated with the self-blame coping strategy (Frydenberg, 2017). While the conceptual dichotomy between 'productive' and 'non-productive' coping is attractively simple and supported by a significant body of research, it must be noted that coping cannot be classified as universally adaptive or maladaptive across all situations, without consideration of personal and situational factors (Matthews, Roberts & Zeidner, 2004). For example, while seeking social support is commonly understood to be a 'productive' coping strategy, if used to excess it could be an indication of dependence rather than a belief in one's own capacities. As such, coping strategies need to be categorised and interpreted with caution, with considerable reference to the individual and the context where possible. There is no right or wrong coping, it is the context in which the actions occur and generally, particularly in the case of adults, it is the self-assessment of the individual that matters. That is, if an adult believes a particular strategy to be helpful they are unlikely to want to desist from using it.

As highlighted in Chapter 2, there are three major contexts that influence development; the family, the school and the community. Each act at times individually and at other times in concert. Whatever innate temperament and capacities the individual may have, the circumstances that surround him or her from birth will provide both the opportunities and the constraints in terms of adaptation. Peers, siblings and teachers are all socialising agents in children's lives that contribute to the development of their coping. However, extensive research has indicated that the family is thought to provide the earliest and most salient context in which children acquire strategies to respond and adapt to stress (e.g. Bradley, 2007; Zimmer-Gembeck & Locke, 2007).

Family structure, that is, who is in the family, family climate and the nature of the interactions in the family, all matter. Parents indirectly and directly influence children's coping strategies, emotional development, prosocial behaviour and empathy, as well as emotion regulation through coaching, modelling and more generally in the family context which includes parenting behaviours and practices (Frydenberg, 2017, 2018). The three parallel pathways, namely, coaching, modelling and family activities, within these developmental frameworks suggest that they are fundamental

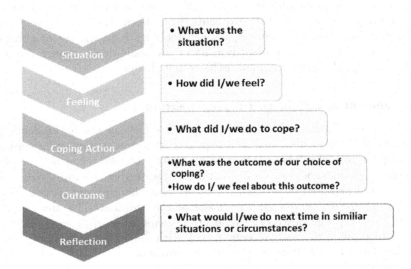

Situation

- What was the situation?

Feeling

- How did I/we feel?

Coping Action

- What did I/we do to cope?

Outcome

- What was the outcome of our choice of coping?
- How do I/ we feel about this outcome?

Reflection

- What would I/we do next time in similiar situations or circumstances?

Figure 5.2 A coping reflection activity

mechanisms by which parents convey important messages to children and influence their behaviour. For example, recent research in mindful parenting shows that parents who bring mindful attention and awareness into their interactions with their children observe more positive behaviours, and less anxiety, depression and acting out in their child (Parent, McKee, Rough & Forehand, 2016). A good starting point for parents would be to first reflect on and examine their own coping. See Figure 5.2, an activity to assist parents or carers of pre-schoolers to reflect on their own coping. When trying to assist individuals in improving their coping skills, the literature highlights the need to increase the use of productive strategies while simultaneously decreasing the use of non-productive strategies (Frydenberg & Lewis, 2002).

What we know about how children cope

Although these taxonomies of coping have been used in research with children and adolescents, the study of coping in children requires a developmental perspective as broad adult-based dimensions of coping are not generally applicable to younger age groups. In a review of 12 coping measures (nine self-report and three observational methods) in paediatric populations by Blount et al., (2008), only six met the criteria of 'well established' that broaden understanding and guide treatment. The authors were focused on how useful the instruments were for intervention. Many of the psychometrically valid instruments have been used exclusively for research rather than intervention, yet the tools lend themselves to clinical applications since the very identification of the individual's coping characteristics can lead to reflection and behavioural change.

Development of a children's coping measure

Similar to the development of the Early Years Coping Cards (Frydenberg & Deans, 2011a) as described in Chapter 4, the development of a coping measure for pre-schoolers is informed by a body of research which sought to expand understandings of the coping capacities of 4- and 5-year-old children and explored how parents' and teachers' descriptions of their children's coping concur and amplify those of the children. The aim was to identify the coping constructs which are relevant to 4- to 5-year-olds and articulate them into a measurement tool with a language of coping that can be related to that used by parents and teachers.

Coping strategies of pre-schoolers

As described in Chapter 4, in Phase I-II of the Early Childhood Research Project, we set out to explore the coping strategies of pre-schoolers, by asking 4-year-old children in Melbourne to describe their coping strategies when dealing with seven age-appropriate challenging situations (Chalmers, Frydenberg & Deans, 2011; Deans, Frydenberg & Tsurutani, 2009). Semi-structured interviews were conducted with 46 4-year-old pre-schoolers using visual images that depicted seven age-appropriate challenging situations described in Chapter 4, namely, being left by a parent, being teased, having to make a choice between friends, trying something new, being told off by a teacher or an adult, being afraid of the dark and being left out by a friend. We wanted to capture the full range of coping strategies described by pre-schoolers and the frequency of use of these different coping strategies across the situations. Children were shown one situation image at a time and asked the following four open-ended questions for each: 1) 'What do you see in this picture?' 2) 'Has this ever happened to you?' If yes, then 3) a) 'How did you feel when this happened to you?' and if no, then b) 'How do you think this person would feel in this situation?' If the child elicited a negative emotion then the question 4) a) 'What would you do to make yourself feel better?' or b) 'What would you say to this person to make them feel better?' was asked. The interviews were more conversational than structured.

The coping responses reported by the pre-schoolers were organised under each of the identified main coping strategies to ensure all the responses were taken into account (Table 5.1, Chalmers et al., 2011). For example, phrases with similar meaning, such as 'I just play' and 'I go away and play somewhere' were placed under the general term 'play' whereas 'get a cuddle from mum' and 'hold my teacher's hand' was defined as 'support seeking'. This list was compared to the list of coping codes generated from the pilot study to form a total of 15 potential coping strategies, namely, 'play/do something else', 'work to solve the problem', 'do nothing/don't know what to do', 'seek comfort', 'think positive', 'cry/can't feel better', 'ignore the problem', 'seek help', 'complain of illness', 'blame others', 'calm down', 'tantrum', 'talk about it', 'keep feelings to self' and 'get angry with self'.

What we have learnt from these studies is that coping strategies reported by children can be clearly clustered into productive and non-productive coping styles as noted in Table 4.1 in Chapter 4. The majority of children can articulate several of the productive coping strategies that

Table 5.1 Coping strategies reported by pre-schoolers for each of the situational cards

Situational Card	Coping Strategy	
Separation from Parents	Play/do something else	
	Seek comfort (pull-up, meds)	
	Do nothing/don't know	
Friendship	Play/do something else	Think positive
	Solve the problem	Ignore problem
	Do nothing/don't know	Seek help
	Seek comfort	
Making a Choice	Play/do something else	
	Solve the problem	
	Do nothing/don't know	
Teacher/Told Off	Play/do something else	Think positive
	Solve the problem	Cry
	Do nothing/don't know	Ignore problem
	Seek comfort	Seek help
	Calm down	Get angry/tantrum
Teasing	Play/do something else	Think positive
	Solve the problem	Seek help
	Do nothing/don't know	Get angry/tantrum
	Seek comfort	
Night Fears	Play/do something else	Cry
	Seek comfort	Ignore problem
	Think positive	Seek help
Don't Like Something	Solve the problem	Ignore problem
	Do nothing/don't know	Seek help
	Think positive	Get angry/tantrum

they can apply across a few different challenging situations. The productive coping strategies are *Play/do something else, Work to solve the problem, Think positive/calm down, Seek comfort, Ignore the problem* and *Seek help*. The non-productive coping strategies include *Do nothing/don't know what to do, Cry/can't feel better, Get angry/tantrum* and *Seek comfort*. Note that some strategies may be productive at times and non-productive at other times, such as *Seek comfort*. That is, sometimes it is helpful and at other times not. For example, it might be a way of calming oneself or a way of avoiding dealing with the problem. Separation anxiety was found to be the most challenging situation for children to apply productive coping skills. Having established a measurement tool, it was then possible to compare parents' and teachers' perceptions of the same child's coping.

Parents' versus teachers' understanding of children's coping

Teachers and parents play a key role in observing children in different settings and can provide a wealth of information about the behaviours of young children. In order to extend understanding on children's coping behaviours in different environments, Deans et al. (2009) matched parents' understandings of their children's coping responses to that of children's using child interviews and an online survey for parents. Parents addressed a list of questions that related specifically to separation, communicative problem-solving, independent problem-solving, social skills and adaptability. Parents were also provided with a list of 27 coping strategies such as 'keep feelings to self' and 'work hard' and asked to rate whether their child used each strategy. We found that the children spontaneously provided more coping strategies than those listed in the parent survey and children also reported using more active coping such as 'just play and pretend', 'just try and fix it' whereas parents would report more passive coping such as 'cry, I would feel sad', 'I would do nothing', compared to their children's responses. What we learnt is that children are capable of comprehending and talking about complex topics and use a language of coping to articulate their thoughts and feelings when provided with the right opportunities and prompts from adults.

Given that parents and teachers have different relationships with the same child, it is expected that observations and perspectives of parents and teachers would differ (Achenbach, McConaughy & Howell, 1987; Gagnon, Nagel & Nickerson, 2007). To examine cross-informant understandings of child coping, Phase III of the research compared parents' and teachers' survey reports of children's use of coping strategies (Frydenberg & Deans, 2011b). The parent and teacher surveys consisted of identical questions relating to general coping, stressors (i.e. types of stressful situations) and situation-specific coping. If a situation was rated applicable for a child, participants were asked to complete it in reference to coping. As shown in Figure 5.3,

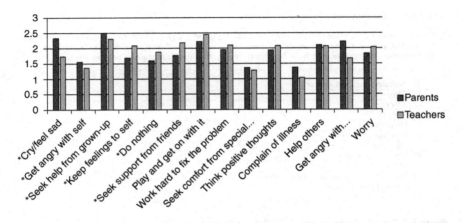

Figure 5.3 Parents' and teachers' mean ratings for children's use of general coping strategies (*significant differences)

differences were found between parents' (44 mothers and 22 fathers) and 4 teachers' ratings of 46 4-year-old children's coping strategies. We found that in this sample, parents' mean ratings for children's use of the strategies Cry, Complain of illness, Seek help from grown-up and Get angry with others/ blame others were significantly greater than teachers' ratings. On the other hand, teachers' mean ratings for Keep feelings to self, Do nothing and Seek support from friends were notably higher than parents' ratings for children's use of these strategies. Moreover, fathers were more likely to rate their children as working hard at solving problems than the mothers.

Variances in parents' perceptions of their children's coping and that of teachers and children themselves might be related to the differences in relationship and perspective as teachers have an opportunity to observe children in the classroom setting and to make peer-group comparisons (Distefano & Kamphaus, 2007). These disparities could also be associated with the number of opportunities the child has to display specific behaviours in certain situations (Ruffalo & Elliott, 1997). Nonetheless, this highlights that parents and teachers can both contribute to creating environments that support productive coping in children.

Three-component model of the Children's Coping Scale

As a result of the previous research mentioned, the Children's Coping Scale – Revised (CCS-R, Yeo, Frydenberg, Northam & Deans, 2014) was developed (see Figure 5.4).

Situation-Specific Coping

Please consider how your child copes when saying goodbye (e.g.going to pre-school, being left with a babysitter, being left at unfamiliar places without a familiar adult) and indicate by checking the appropriate box, how frequently your child uses a particular coping strategy.

	Never	Sometimes	A Lot
1. Notice what others are doing			
2. Play			
3. Try			
4. Worry			
5. Do nothing			
6. Give up			
7. Chat to friends			
8. Cry or scream			
9. Hope			
10. Keep feelings to self / not show how he/she feels			
11. Try to help others			

Figure 5.4 Sample items on the CCS-R for situation-specific coping[1]

The CCS-R consists of 29 child-specific coping strategies (e.g. 'Get a teacher or grown-up to help') which teachers and parents could rate on a three-point Likert scale (Never, Sometimes, A Lot). Parents or teachers could rate the 29 coping strategies across general coping and/or specific situations such as when their child has to say goodbye or has to do something he/she does not like.

In order to identify the coping dimensions in 4- and 5-year-olds, Yeo et al. (2014) conducted a factor analytic study using the CCS-R with larger sample (N=94). Parents were asked to rate their child's use of 29 coping strategies in general and in two specific situations (i.e. separating from parents; being asked to do something s/he does not like). Based on the parents' responses about their child's coping in general, a three-component model was generated which included Positive Coping, Negative Coping – Emotional Expression and Negative Coping – Emotional Inhibition. Positive Coping consisted of both problem-focused/primary-control strategies (i.e. those that involved active efforts to try to solve the problem through managing or modifying the situation, e.g., 'try') and emotion-focused/secondary-control strategies (i.e. those that managed or reduced any emotional distress by adapting to the situation, e.g., 'be happy with the way things are', 'have fun, go out and play and forget about their problem'). The two Negative Coping components were mostly emotion-focused; the difference being whether the emotions were overtly expressed (Emotional Expression, e.g., 'worry', 'cry or scream', 'keep away

---

1 All items are listed in Table 5.2.

from other children') or covertly expressed (Emotional Inhibition, e.g., 'keep feelings to self/not show how s/he feels', 'do nothing'). This distinction, however, was not necessarily clear for some coping behaviours (e.g. while worry loaded onto Emotional Expression, it can be considered an internalising behaviour and could be argued to be similar to Emotional Inhibition; however, it can also be regarded as a form of Emotional Expression given that worries can be openly discussed with others). Emotional Expression and Emotional Inhibition were labelled as Negative Coping because they included behaviours and emotions found to be distressing to children and parents.

This three-component model (Table 5.2) was confirmed by Pang et al. (2015) when additional parents were combined with data from a previous study. The similar number of coping dimensions derived for pre-schoolers in these studies gives increased confidence to the finding that distinct dimensions of pre-schoolers' coping may be developmentally different from coping patterns in later years. Moreover, the distinction between Emotional Expression and Emotional Inhibition in pre-schoolers' coping behaviour may not always be clear (e.g. worry could be both a form of internalisation and a form of expression). Nonetheless, the conceptualisation of two distinct emotion-focused coping dimensions for pre-schoolers gives greater insight into the coping patterns and strategies that pre-schoolers might employ to deal with the stressors they experience.

In 2017, Kiernan, Frydenberg, Deans and Liang extended these findings by replicating the three-component structure of coping in a sample of 132 pre-schoolers (Positive Coping, Negative Coping – Emotional Expression and Negative Coping – Emotional Inhibition) as measured by the CCS-R (parents' reports) not only for the General Coping form but also the two Situation-Specific Coping forms (Saying Goodbye and Dislike). Findings from this study confirmed that the three-component model was the best fit for both General and Situation-Specific Coping. Moreover, the two situation-specific forms were both more reliable and loaded more consistently with previous research than the General Coping Form, suggesting that salience or relevance matters when assessing coping. Additionally, the Goodbye Form was the most reliable which could imply that saying goodbye was a more relevant concern for pre-schoolers than the more general scenario of disliking something. This proposition is supported by research that suggests that saying goodbye, or separation from a parent, is a very common concern for pre-schoolers (Chalmers et al., 2011; Frydenberg & Deans, 2011b). The implication of these studies is that if only one measure of coping is feasible for a pre-schooler, an assessment of situation-specific coping based on a child's most salient issue may be the most accurate measure of coping for that pre-schooler.

The Children's Coping Scale – Revised has been validated across different studies. The validity of a tool or measurement instrument is achieved

Table 5.2 Rotated component loadings for the three-component model of the Children's Coping Scale – Revised (Pang, Frydenberg & Deans, 2015)

	Component		
Coping Scale Items	Positive	Negative –Emotional Expression	Negative –Emotional Inhibition
Have fun, play sport, draw, play games	.81		
Play	.71		
Chat to friends	.69		
Work with others	.68		
Work hard	.66		
Try to help others	.63		
Be happy with the way things are	.61		
Hope	.56		
Spend a lot of time with a good friend	.56		
Go out and play and forget about their problem	.55		
Try	.53		
Notice what others are doing	.51		
Get a teacher or grown-up to help	.42		
'Lose it' – cry, scream or fight		.75	
Cry or scream		.73	
Feel sad		.66	
Get angry with others		.49	
Keep away from other children		.47	
Feel bad		.45	
Blame themselves/when things go wrong		.42	
Worry		.42	
Get mad with themselves		.36	
Keep feelings to self/not show how he/she feels			.65
Do nothing			.56
Don't let others know how they are feeling			.55
Get stomach aches or headaches			.54
Give up			.53
Get sick			.53
Ask a teacher for help			.42

Note. Loadings of components retained in the final three-component solution are in boldface.

in a number of ways, but the general principle is that the validity of a construct is established through an association with another construct that has been measured. For example, the association between anxiety and non-productive coping. In Chapter 6 the correlates of coping are considered along with the implications for the measurement of mental health.

Take home messages

- We can measure coping in adult, adolescent and child populations through self-reports or for children through parent and/or teacher reports.
- What people report doing at a particular time with a particular problem may vary according to the occasion and circumstances and they can always change their coping. Therefore, it is not helpful to label people according to their coping.
- Adults are encouraged to reflect on their coping as are children.
- Children as young as 3 and 4 can identify emotions and can describe how they cope. We can identify coping in the early years in a reliable and valid way.
- Children's coping actions can be categorised into positive and negative with negative coping being identified as Negative Coping Emotional Inhibition and Negative Coping Emotional Expression.
- There is no right or wrong coping but the helpfulness or unhelpfulness of a strategy can be considered in a particular context.
- Parents and teachers describe the same child's coping in different ways and children have different perspectives on their own coping than parents and teachers.
- Measurement of coping is helpful as a way of describing an individual's behaviour. It may provide understanding, reflection and stimulate a desire to make a change.

References

Achenbach, T. M., McConaughy, S. H., & Howell, C. T. (1987). Child/Adolescent behavioral and emotional problems: Implications of cross-informant correlations and situational specificity. *Psychological Bulletin, 101*(2), 213–232.

Blount, R. L., Simons, L. E., Devine, K. A., Jaaniste, T., Cohen, L. L., Chambers, C. T., & Hayutin, L. G. (2008). Evidence-based assessment of coping and stress in pediatric psychology. *Journal Of Pediatric Psychology, 33*(9), 1021–1045. doi:10.1093/jpepsy/jsm071

Bradley, R. H. (2007). Parenting in the breach: How parents help children cope with developmentally challenging circumstances. *Parenting: Science and Practice, 7*, 99–148.

Chalmers, K., Frydenberg, E., & Deans, J. (2011). An exploration into the coping strategies of pre-schoolers: Implications for professional practice. *Children Australia, 36*, 120–127.

Deans, J., Frydenberg, E., & Tsurutani, H. (2009). *Operationalising social and emotional coping competencies in pre-school children.* Paper presented at New Zealand Research Early Childhood Research Conference, Wellington.

Distefano, C. A., & Kamphaus, R. W. (2007). Development and validation of a behavioral screener for pre-school-age children. *Journal of Emotional and Behavioral Disorders, 15*(2), 93–102.

Frydenberg, E. (2017). *Coping and the challenge of resilience.* London: Palgrave Macmillan.

Frydenberg, E. (2018). *Adolescent coping: Promoting resilience and wellbeing.* U.K.: Routledge.

Frydenberg, E., & Deans, J. (2011a). *The Early Years Coping Cards.* Melbourne: Australian Council for Educational Research.

Frydenberg, E., & Deans, J. (2011b). Coping competencies in the early years: Identifying the strategies that pre-schoolers use. In P. Buchenwald & K. Moore (Eds.) Proceedings of STAR Conference 2010. 17–26.

Frydenberg, E., & Lewis, R. (1997). *Coping Scale for Adults.* Melbourne: Australian Council for Educational Research.

Frydenberg, E., & Lewis, R. (2002). Do managers cope productively? A comparison between Australian middle level managers and adults in the general community. *Journal of Managerial Psychology, 17,* 640–654.

Frydenberg, E., & Lewis, R. (2014). *Coping Scale for Adults – second edition (CSA-2).* Melbourne: Australian Council for Educational Research.

Gagnon, S. G., Nagel, R. J., & Nickerson, A. B. (2007). Parent and teacher ratings of peer interactive play and social-emotional development of pre-school children at risk. *Journal of Early Intervention, 29*(3), 228–242.

Kiernan, N., Frydenberg, E., Deans, J., & Liang, R. (2017). The relationship between parent-reported coping, stress, and mental health in a pre-school population. *Educational and Developmental Psychologist, 34*(2), 124–141.

Lazarus, R. S., & Folkman, S. (1984). *Stress, appraisal, and coping.* New York: Springer.

Matthews, G., Roberts, R. D., & Zeidner, M. (2004). Seven myths about emotional intelligence. *Psychological Inquiry, 15*(3), 179–196.

Pang, I., Frydenberg, E., & Deans, J. (2015). The relationship between anxiety and coping in pre-schoolers. In P. Buchenwald & K. Moore (Eds.), *Anxiety, stress & coping* (pp. 26–27). Berlin: Verlag.

Parent, J., McKee, L. G., Rough, J. N., & Forehand, R. (2016). The association of parent mindfulness with parenting and youth psychopathology across three developmental stages. *Journal of Abnormal Child Psychology, 44*(1), 191–202. doi:10.1007/s10802-015-9978-x

Ruffalo, S. L., & Elliott, S. N. (1997). Teachers' and parents' ratings of children's social skills: A closer look at cross-informant agreements through an item analysis protocol. *School Psychology Review, 26*(3), 489–502.

Yeo, K., Frydenberg, E., Northam, E., & Deans, J. (2014). Coping with stress among pre-school children and associations with anxiety level and controllability of situations. *Australian Journal of Psychology, 66,* 93–101. doi:10.1111/ajpy.12047

Zimmer-Gembeck, M. J., & Locke, E. M. (2007). The socialization of adolescent coping behaviors: Relationships with families and teachers. *Journal of Adolescence, 30,* 1–16.

Chapter 6

The relationship between coping, stress and mental health in a pre-school population

'When people sit together they make each other smile and they help if someone is sad.'
~ Eugene, 5-year-old

Overview

Building on the previous chapter, Chapter 6 explores the relationship between coping, stress and common mental health issues facing the pre-school population through the use of Children's Coping Scale – Revised (CCS-R) in association with indicators of children's anxiety and social emotional competence. It highlights the importance of using a developmental approach to understand general versus situation-specific coping responses in pre-schoolers, including a discussion on the early patterns of maladaptive coping among anxious pre-schoolers. Implications for early mental health prevention and intervention are considered.

Coping and mental health: a developmental perspective

As defined in the early chapters, coping skills are strategies, comprised of thoughts, feelings and actions, that help people to deal with challenging situations encountered in everyday life and in particular circumstances in order to achieve positive mental health and well-being. The research on coping and mental health is unequivocal: how a person copes with stress impacts their mental health and psychological adjustment (Compas, Connor-Smith, Saltzman, Thomsen & Wadsworth, 2001; Frydenberg & Lewis, 2009; Holen, Lervåg, Waaktaar & Ystgaard, 2012; Wright, Banerjee, Hoek, Rieffe & Novin, 2010). Conversely, having good mental health and well-being can impact how one copes (see Figure 1.1).

Coping skills take many forms and they change throughout and in parallel to the development of a child across time. From both the ecological and coping perspectives, *challenges* are features of the environment, including daily demands and difficulties, as well as developmental tasks and major life events, that tax or are beyond a child's <u>current</u> coping capacity. As a child develops and encounters more challenges in life, with the consistent support, guidance and healthy boundaries set by the adults in their life, they will learn to acquire and utilise more prosocial ways of coping (Bronfenbrenner, 1979; Moreland & Dumas, 2008).

In early development, all young children cope with challenges in prosocial, antisocial or asocial ways which serve an important role in survival and attachment. For example, an infant might cry to signal discomfort or hunger; a toddler might avoid strangers or unfamiliar situations to prevent themselves from getting into danger. Angry outbursts are expressions of affect that precede the young child's ability to express emotions in more appropriate ways in response to challenging social situations (Moreland & Dumas, 2008). Changes in coping are prevalent from infancy through to adulthood, during which the structure, organisation and flexibility in coping processes are likely to undergo significant changes. Researchers in the field (Skinner & Zimmer-Gembeck, 2007; Skinner & Zimmer-Gembeck, 2009) have found that coping developed most rapidly during childhood (ages 5 to 7) and during transition to adolescence (ages 8 to 12). The presence of these developmental shifts in coping suggests broad developmental phases that are characterised by different mechanisms of regulation and differing involvement by social partners such as family and peers. Overall, these studies suggest that coping is more malleable during childhood and more trait-like and stable in adulthood. This calls for an attention and focus for parents, carers and educators to facilitate the acquisition and development of healthy coping skills in young children – through modelling and active coaching.

Research on children's coping and mental health

Research on the relationship between coping and mental health in children, particularly for pre-schoolers, is limited. Very few of these studies have focused on general mental health; most studies have focused on either general well-being (Frydenberg & Lewis, 2009), clinical samples or children with a disability or depression and anxiety (Babb, Levine & Arseneault, 2010; Dahlbeck & Lightsey, 2008; Hema et al., 2009; Miller et al., 2009; Thompson et al., 2010; Wright et al., 2010). The prevalence of child mental health disorders such as anxiety and associated comorbidities is similar to that seen in later childhood (Egger & Angold, 2006). In a meta-review of coping and mental health in children and adolescents, Compas and colleagues (2001) found that engagement coping and problem-focused coping were associated with more positive adjustment. The coping subtypes most often associated with positive adjustment were problem-solving, cognitive restructuring and positive reappraisal of the stressors. These strategies reflect an ability to carefully analyse and problem-solve a situation, the ability to focus on the positives during times of stress and also the ability to generate alternative, more helpful thoughts about a situation. In contrast, disengagement coping and emotion-focused coping were related to poorer adjustment. Specific coping strategies associated with poorer adjustment include avoidance (cognitive and behavioural), social withdrawal, resigned acceptance, emotional venting, wishful thinking and self-blame/self-criticism (Compas et al., 2001). Additionally, their research also indicates that context matters. In situations such as parental conflict or sexual abuse where the stressor was subjectively or objectively uncontrollable by the child, engagement and problem-focused coping were associated with poorer adjustment. This suggests as one would expect that direct problem-solving or engagement with a stressor may be ineffective in situations outside a child's control.

Consensus from longitudinal developmental and clinical studies support the claim that children exhibiting high levels of prosocial coping and low levels of antisocial and asocial coping are better able to deal with normative and stressful life challenges. For example, Halpern (2004) found that pre-schoolers who used more problem-focused approach coping had greater psychological adjustment while children with more no-coping responses had higher internalising and externalising scores as measured by the Child Behaviour Checklist (CBCL; Achenbach, 1991, 1992). The children who use a more problem-solving approach tend also to follow more adaptive developmental trajectories than children with limited coping skills (Kohlberg, 1984; Moreland & Dumas, 2008; Valiente, Lemery-Chalfant & Swanson, 2009; Wadsworth, Raviv, Compas & Connor-Smith, 2005).

Relationships between coping, prosocial and problem behaviours

It has long been established that we can improve children's long-term well-being by preventing antisocial behaviour and promoting prosocial behaviour in their early years (Hudson & Buchanan, 2000). Improving prosocial skills and reducing problem behaviours are common objectives of SEL programs (see Chapter 3) as they are important elements of children's social emotional functioning. There is longstanding evidence that quality SEL interventions are effective in fostering prosocial behaviours while reducing problem behaviours such as conduct and emotional problems (Durlak, Weissberg, Dymnicki, Taylor & Schellinger, 2011; Payton et al., 2008). Fewer conduct problems and improved prosocial behaviour reflects mastery of SEL competencies (Greenberg et al., 2003). Prosocial behaviour can be defined as behaviours involving intention to benefit others and foster positive social interactions (Eisenberg, Fabes & Spinrad, 2006) such as comfort, sharing, cooperating or helping others (Williams & Berthelsen, 2017). Problem behaviours refer to a broad array of behavioural issues that are not conducive to well-being or learning, which might include hyperactivity, social problems, emotional symptoms and conduct problems (Goodman, 1997).

Levels of prosocial and problematic behaviours in a child are commonly measured by the Strengths and Difficulties Questionnaire for 4 to 10 years old (SDQ; Goodman, 2001). The SDQ is a brief screening instrument for child and adolescent mental health and is used widely in both clinical and community-based research (Goodman, Ford, Simmons, Gatward & Meltzer, 2003; Vostanis, 2006; Woerner et al., 2004). The SDQ is comprised of 25 questions which parents rate on a three-point Likert scale (Not True, Somewhat True, Certainly True) and the results typically derive five dimensions of children's mental health: Emotional Symptoms, Conduct Problems, Hyperactivity/Inattention, Peer Problems and Prosocial Behaviour. One study (Kiernan, Frydenberg, Deans & Liang, 2017) explored the relationship between different coping patterns and mental health (as measured by the Strengths and Difficulties Questionnaire; SDQ) in a sample of 132 preschoolers. Correlational analyses were conducted to explore the relationships between types of coping (e.g. Positive Coping, Negative Coping – Emotional Expression and Negative Coping – Emotional Inhibition as mentioned in Chapter 5) and mental health; with mental health measured by the subscales of the SDQ (e.g. Emotional Symptoms, Conduct Problems, Hyperactivity/Inattention, Peer Problems and Prosocial Behaviour).

The relationships between anxiety and coping in young children

Anxiety in pre-schoolers

Fearful and anxious behaviour is common in young children particularly when they are yet to learn to cope with new situations and experiences. However, some children react more quickly or intensely to situations they find threatening, or find it harder to get their anxious feelings under control. It is a concern when anxiety stops them from participating in activities at school or socially. Anxiety disorders are widely acknowledged as the most prevalent class of psychiatric illness during the pre-school period with most studies estimating the prevalence of pre-school anxiety disorders in the range of 10% to 20%. The variation likely reflects differences in assessment tools (clinical interview, parental report, direct observation), geographic location and demographic differences between study samples (Whalen, Sylvester & Luby, 2017). The four most common anxiety disorders experienced in the pre-school period are:

i   Separation anxiety disorder (excessive fear surrounding separation from caregivers)
ii   Social phobia (excessive fear of negative social evaluation)
iii Generalised anxiety disorder (excessive anxious anticipation of future events)
iv   Specific phobia (excessive fear of specific stimuli, such as dogs or heights)

Gender differences in anxiety do not seem to be strong in young children, although they may emerge with increasing age (Spence, Rapee, McDonald & Ingram, 2001), around the ages of 4 to 5 (Roza, Hofstra, van der Ende & Verhulst, 2003). Recent studies also found no differences in the anxiety levels or the utilisation of the various coping dimensions across gender for the pre-schoolers (Pang, Frydenberg & Deans, 2015; Yeo, Frydenberg, Northam & Deans, 2014).

Within anxiety research, it is well established that avoidance is a central feature of anxiety in children (Baldwin & Dadds, 2007; Beesdo, Knappe & Pine, 2009). There are several mechanisms by which avoidant behaviours may develop into a characteristic coping style for anxious children. Research indicates that anxious children tend to have a behaviourally inhibited temperament that manifests in observable behaviours such as refraining from exploration and approaching other children (Biederman et al., 2001; Kagan, 1997). As temperament is largely stable (Kagan, Snidman, Arcus & Reznick, 1994; Sanson, Pedlow, Cann, Prior & Oberklaid, 1996), these early behavioural responses to unfamiliar situations form the template for avoidant coping in stressful situations in later life. Second, there is also evidence that parents of anxious children may foster an avoidant approach to stressful situations (Barrett, Rapee, Dadds & Ryan, 1996; McClure, Brennan, Hammen & Le Brocque, 2001). These studies introduce an interesting empirical question of whether anxious children are more inclined towards emotion-focused, passive/inhibited, withdrawal types of coping, as opposed to problem-focused and active/approach response styles.

Parent as informants of child coping and child anxiety

Parents can provide a critical perspective on children's functioning and are perhaps the most widely-used informants, offering judgements that are idiographic and unique to the child (Konold, Brewster & Pianta, 2004). One of the common parent-reported anxiety measures for pre-schoolers is the Spence Pre-school Anxiety Scale (SPAS, Spence et al., 2001). It contains a list of 34 symptoms of anxiety (e.g. 'afraid of meeting unfamiliar people' and 'spends a large part of each day worrying') where parents are asked to rate how true each symptom is of their child on a five-point Likert scale. Although not being a diagnostic tool, SPAS provides a measure of children's total level of anxiety along with their generalised anxiety, social anxiety, obsessive-compulsive anxiety, specific fears and separation anxiety. Information from the SPAS and that of the Children's Coping Scale – Revised: Parent Rating Form (see Chapter 5 for more details on CCS-R) which measures children's positive and negative coping styles (Emotional Inhibition/Emotional Expression) in general and in two specific situations (saying goodbye; doing something s/he does not like), allows researchers to investigate the relationship between a child's level of anxiety and their coping mechanisms (e.g. Pang et al., 2015; Yeo et al., 2014). Findings in these studies reveal that pre-schoolers (N=119) can use positive coping strategies to cope with stressors regardless of their level of anxiety. However, those who were rated higher on anxiety were more likely to engage in negative forms of coping, specifically using emotionally expressive coping strategies that may be less adaptive. Children who were rated as more anxious by their parents were more likely to use an emotion-focused way of coping, with a predominant focus on the expression of negative emotions or coping through behaviours akin to withdrawal and giving up.

Relationship between coping styles and anxiety types

Building on Yeo's and Pang's studies, Cornell and colleagues (2017) further investigated whether the situation and the anxiety type make a difference to the relationship between coping and anxiety in pre-schoolers (N=72). The study examined the relationships between each of the coping styles and anxiety types across different situations and identified which of the coping styles uniquely contributed to each specific anxiety type. Similar to previous studies, higher levels of rated anxiety in pre-schoolers were observed for higher levels of Negative Coping. However, this study revealed that different styles of coping were used by pre-schoolers across specific situations. Although the relationship between coping and generalised anxiety varies across the situations, a clear pattern emerged for social anxiety with children engaging in more Negative Coping – Emotional Inhibition. For separation anxiety, the relationship between coping and anxiety was only found in the goodbye specific situation with children engaging in more Negative Coping – Emotional Expression. These findings suggest that coping styles can vary according to the situation and the anxiety experienced, suggesting it is important to go beyond children's experiences of general coping styles and overall anxiety.

Bi-directional relationship between coping and anxiety

The relationship between anxiety and a tendency to engage in negative forms of coping may be bi-directional (Seiffge-Krenke, 2000). Temperament is defined as early-appearing, trait-like individual differences in emotional, attentional and motor reactivity to novel stimuli, measured by latency, intensity and recovery of response, and self-regulation processes (Rothbart & Derryberry, 1981). It is the initial state from which personality develops and links individual differences in behaviour to underlying neural networks. Temperament and experiences together enable a child to develop cognitions about self, others and the physical and social world, as well as his or her values, attitudes and coping strategies (Rothbart, 2007). In their review paper, Whalen et al. (2017) suggested that Behavioural Inhibition (BI), a temperament characterised by high reactivity and negative emotional response to novel stimuli (e.g. strangers or new toys), is one of the most potent known risk factors for developing an anxiety disorder across the life-span, including during the pre-school period. Children who are temperamentally anxious may possess less flexibility in modifying their coping responses and are predisposed towards maladaptive coping which may in turn exacerbate pre-existing anxiety. These children tend to have a heightened attentional capacity for threatening situations, to appraise ambiguous situations in threatening ways and to overestimate threat in situations (Hadwin, Garner & Perez-Olivas, 2006; Rapee, Schniering & Hudson, 2009). These cognitive appraisals and beliefs may foster a sense of lack of control in the events of their lives even when situations may be more controllable than they perceive. The implication is that these children might rely mostly on avoidance responses in anxiety-provoking situations and be unwilling to employ approach strategies (Rapee, 2002). They tend also to underestimate their ability to cope in anxiety-provoking situations (Dadds & Barrett, 2001; Suveg & Zeman, 2004) and rely on maladaptive ways of coping. Over time, they might develop an overreliance on avoidant or emotion-focused coping, thus limiting their ability to flexibly utilise the range of coping strategies demonstrated by non-anxious age peers.

If the relationship is indeed bi-directional, improving children's coping may have a direct effect on reducing anxiety. Some researchers have suggested that as children grow older, temperament factors (such as a tendency to be anxious) may play a less important role as children develop greater capacities for self-regulation of cognition, behaviour and emotion in response to stress (e.g. Compas, 1998). However, a recent longitudinal study indicated that anxious children (aged 8 to 11 years old) exhibited increased coping through withdrawal over a nine-month period (Wright et al., 2010). Further longitudinal research may shed more light on the relationship between coping and anxiety. Despite this, it remains important that children be encouraged and taught to develop positive coping strategies and avoid developing negative coping patterns (Frydenberg, Deans & O'Brien, 2012). Based on learning and cognitive theories for both coping and anxiety, anxious pre-schoolers could be expected to learn effective coping strategies (Frydenberg et al., 2012; Rachman, 1998). If a child believes s/he has strategies to cope effectively then the impact of anxiety on normal functioning may be lowered.

Parental influence on pre-schoolers' anxiety and coping

Anxiety and coping are also shaped by social relationships and contexts such as the family environment. The environment in which coping occurs may be regarded as a potential resource or constraint that influences coping (Frydenberg & Lewis, 2002). Research has found that parental anxiety could be associated with pre-school anxiety through genetic transmission, parenting techniques, observation of parental anxiety or other mechanisms (Field & Lawson, 2003). For example, parents of anxious children were more likely to model, prompt and reinforce maladaptive coping strategies such as avoidance and distress in stressful situations (Donovan & Spence, 2000). In particular, parental negative affect was one of the potential risk factors for anxiety in children aged 4 to 6, where children inherited an increased propensity to develop non-specific anxiety problems (Pahl, Barrett & Gullo, 2012). Parents of anxious children tended also to be overprotective and were more critical of the child's coping attempts (Krohne & Hock, 1991). They were also more likely than parents of non-clinical and aggressive children to reciprocate their child's avoidant coping strategies and were less likely to encourage prosocial solutions to cope with stressful situations that are ambiguous (Rapee et al., 2009). The use of maladaptive coping strategies in children may be reinforced if their parents failed to help them learn adequate coping strategies because these parents may model anxious behaviours themselves and may display over-controlling parenting styles (Morren, Muris, Kindt, Schouten & van Den Hout, 2008). Hence, such parenting behaviours may influence the child's own coping attempts and skill development when dealing with developmentally stressful events independently.

The role of controllability: situation matters

Pre-schoolers' development and utilisation of various coping strategies can also be influenced by the level of controllability of the stressful situation on their coping. Controllability of the situation was first investigated by Lazarus and Folkman (1984) in their conceptualisation of problem- and emotion-focused coping. Controllability refers to how much an individual believes that he/she has the ability to exert objective control over the event. Lazarus and Folkman (1984) suggested that when the stressor is controllable, adults tend to use problem-focused coping whereas when the stressor is uncontrollable, emotion-focused coping predominates. Band and Weisz (1988) were among the first investigators to report that pre-schoolers evidenced a similar ability to use different coping strategies in response to different situations. They found that 6-year-old children tend to use more primary coping in controllable situations (e.g. separation from a friend, peer difficulty and school failure) than in less controllable situations (e.g. medical procedures or physical accidents). This finding was replicated in later research with pre-schoolers (Chalmers, Frydenberg & Deans, 2011; Pincus & Friedman, 2004). Chalmers et al. (2011) found that situations in which pre-schoolers generated most primary-control coping strategies included 'being left out of a game', 'choosing between friends' and 'choosing between things that the child doesn't like' as opposed to situations in which secondary control predominated such as 'night fears' and 'being told off by the teacher'. Thus, it appears that pre-schoolers were able to discriminate between situations and differentially utilise coping strategies. Yeo et al. (2014) investigated this concept of controllability and it is applicable to the pre-school population. A series of analyses were conducted to determine the relationships between anxiety and controllability for each of the three coping dimensions as mentioned earlier: Positive Coping, Negative Coping – Emotional Expression and Emotional Inhibition. The same set of coping strategies were presented for situation-specific questions in which parents rated how often the child used each of the strategies in two different situations – separating from parents and being asked to do something he/she doesn't like. These two situations were selected as they were common stressful situations for this population of children. In addition, they are thought to represent a low-control situation (separating from parents) and a high-control situation (doing something he/she doesn't like). Results from this study show children used more Positive Coping and less Negative Coping, both Emotional Expression and Emotional Inhibition, in a low-control situation than in a high-control situation.

Contrary to adult and adolescent models, pre-schoolers in Yeo's sample in general were more likely to use Negative Coping in a more controllable situation and to use Positive Coping in a less controllable situation. Possible explanations for these findings include: (i) it is hard to operationalise the concept of controllability in the pre-school population, partly because one cannot ask young children to independently rate situations on controllability; (ii) the difference in pre-schoolers' coping may not be differentiated on the basis of the level of control, as young children may simply have difficulty judging the controllability of a situation (Compas, 1998; Fields & Prinz, 1997); and (iii) the process of matching coping strategies with the controllability of a stressor is a complex one which might be hard to grasp for children in this developmental stage.

Nonetheless, studies on children with parents in conflict have demonstrated that the use of problem-focused coping (such as intervening in parental conflict) increased children's risk for adjustment problems (Jenkins, Smith & Graham, 1989; Nicolotti, El-Sheikh & Whitson, 2003) while avoidance coping appeared to be a buffer for adjustment problems (Kerig, 2001; O'Brien, Bahadur, Gee, Balto & Erber, 1997). Some authors have suggested that when problem-focused or primary-control coping was applied to uncontrollable events (such as parental conflict), it increased psychological distress because these strategies were likely to be ineffective. Conversely, the use of emotion-focused or secondary control in non-modifiable events fostered a sense of acceptance and vicarious control, which restored a sense of well-being (Compas, 1998; Frydenberg & Deans, 2011). This suggested that the use of primary-control or problem-focused coping is context dependent and not always associated with positive psychosocial outcomes.

Children who are most effective at coping with stressful situations are those who not only possess a repertoire of coping strategies, but who are also able to differentiate between controllable and uncontrollable situations and then flexibly apply different strategies to different situations.

In sum, Yeo et al. (2014) and Pang et al. (2015) found that pre-schoolers rated higher on anxiety were more likely to engage in Negative Coping, particularly Negative Emotional Expression, while pre-schoolers rated lower on anxiety used more positive forms of coping. These findings and the distinctions in Emotional Expression and Emotional Inhibition coping responses in pre-schoolers highlight the importance of a developmental approach to coping research and an early pattern of maladaptive coping among anxious pre-schoolers, which has implications for early mental health prevention and intervention.

Take home messages

- Anxiety in children is now accepted as a phenomenon of childhood as it is for adolescents and adults.
- The relationships between anxiety and coping is bidirectional.
- Teach coping skills to resource young people to deal with not only familiar situations but also unexpected ones.

References

Achenbach, T. M. (1991). *Manual for the child behavior checklist/4–18 and 1991 profile*. Burlington, VT: University of Vermont Department of Psychiatry.

Achenbach, T. M. (1992). *Manual for the child behavior checklist/2–3 and 1992 profile*. Burlington, VT: University of Vermont Department of Psychiatry.

Babb, K. A., Levine, L. J., & Arseneault, J. M. (2010). Shifting gears: Coping flexibility in children with and without ADHD. *International Journal of Behavioral Development, 34*(1), 10–23.

Baldwin, J. S., & Dadds, M. R. (2007). Reliability and validity of parent and child versions of the multidimensional anxiety scale for children in community samples. *Journal of the American Academy of Child and Adolescent Psychiatry, 46*(2), 252–260.

Band, E. B., & Weisz, J. R. (1988). How to feel better when it feels bad: Children's perspectives on coping with everyday stress. *Developmental Psychology, 24* (2), 247–253.

Barrett, P. M., Rapee, R. M., Dadds, M. M., & Ryan, S. M. (1996). Family enhancement of cognitive style in anxious and aggressive children. *Journal of Abnormal Child Psychology, 24*(2), 187–203.

Beesdo, K., Knappe, S., & Pine, D. S. (2009). Anxiety and anxiety disorders in children and adolescents: Developmental issues and implications for DSM-V. *The Psychiatric Clinics of North America, 32*(3), 483–524.

Biederman, J., Hirshfeld-Becker, D. R., Rosenbaum, J. F., Herot, C., Friedman, D., Snidman, N., … Faraone, S. V. (2001). Further evidence of association between behavioral inhibition and social anxiety in children. *The American Journal of Psychiatry, 158*(10), 1673–1979.

Bronfenbrenner, U. (1979). Contexts of child rearing: Problems and prospects. *American Psychologist, 34*, 844–850.

Chalmers, K., Frydenberg, E., & Deans, J. (2011). An exploration into the coping strategies of pre-schoolers: Implications for professional practice. *Children Australia, 36*, 120–127.

Compas, B. E. (1998). An agenda for coping research and theory: Basic and applied developmental issues. *International Journal of Behavioral Development, 22*, 231–237.

Compas, B. E., Connor-Smith, J. K., Saltzman, H., Thomsen, A. H., & Wadsworth, M. E. (2001). Coping with stress during childhood and adolescence: Problems, progress, and potential in theory and research. *Psychological Bulletin, 127*(1), 87–127.

Cornell, C., Kiernan, N., Kaufman, D., Dobeee, P., Frydenberg, E., & Deans, J. (2017). Developing social emotional competence in the early years. In E. Frydenberg, A. J. Martin, & R. J. Collie (Eds.), *Social and Emotional Learning in Australia and the Asia-Pacific* (pp. 391–441). Singapore: Springer.

Dadds, M. R., & Barrett, P. M. (2001). Practitioner review: Psychological management of anxiety disorders in childhood. *Journal of Child Psychology and Psychiatry, 42*(8), 999–1011.

Dahlbeck, D. T., & Lightsey, O. R., Jr. (2008). Generalized self-efficacy, coping, and self-esteem as predictors of psychological adjustment among children with disabilities or chronic illnesses. *Children's Health Care, 37*, 293–315.

Donovan, C. L., & Spence, S. H. (2000). Prevention of childhood anxiety disorders. *Clinical Psychology Review, 20*(4), 509–531.

Durlak, J. A., Weissberg, R. P., Dymnicki, A. B., Taylor, R. D., & Schellinger, K. B. (2011). The impact of enhancing students' social and emotional learning: A meta-analysis of school-based universal interventions. *Child Development, 82*(1), 405–432. doi:10.1111/j.1467-8624.2010.01564.x

Egger, H. L., & Angold, A. (2006). Common emotional and behavioral disorders in pre-school children: Presentation, nosology, and epidemiology. *Journal of Child Psychology and Psychiatry, 47*, 313–337.

Eisenberg, N., Fabes, R. A., & Spinrad, T. L. (2006). Prosocial development. In W. Damon & R. Lerner (Eds.), *Handbook of child psychology, social, emotional, and personality development* (Vol. 3, pp. 646–702). Hoboken, NJ: John Wiley & Sons.

Field, A. P., & Lawson, J. (2003). Fear information and the development of fears during childhood: Effects on implicit fear responses and behavioural avoidance. *Behaviour Research And Therapy, 41*(11), 1277.

Fields, L., & Prinz, R. J. (1997). Coping and adjustment during childhood and adolescence. *Clinical Psychology Review*, *17*, 937–976.

Frydenberg, E., & Deans, J. (2011). Coping competencies in the early years: Identifying the strategies that pre-schoolers use. In P. Buchwald, K. A. Moore, & T. Ringeisen (Eds.), *Stress and anxiety: Application to education and health* (pp. 17–26). Berlin: Logos.

Frydenberg, E., Deans, J., & O'Brien, K. (2012). *Developing everyday coping skills in the early years: Proactive strategies for supporting social and emotional development.* New York, NY: Continuum International.

Frydenberg, E., & Lewis, R. (2002). Do managers cope productively? A comparison between Australian middle level managers and adults in the general community. *Journal Of Managerial Psychology*, *17*, 640–654.

Frydenberg, E., & Lewis, R. (2009). Relations among well-being, avoidant coping, and active coping in a large sample of Australian adolescents. *Psychological Reports*, *104*, 745–758.

Goodman, R. (1997). The strengths and difficulties questionnaire: A research note. *Journal of Child Psychology and Psychiatry*, *38*, 581–586. doi:10.1111/j.1469-7610.1997.tb01545.x

Goodman, R. (2001). Psychometric properties of the strengths and difficulties questionnaire. *Journal of the American Academy of Child & Adolescent Psychiatry*, *40* (11), 1337–1345.

Goodman, R., Ford, T., Simmons, H., Gatward, R., & Meltzer, H. (2003). Using the Strengths and Difficulties Questionnaire (SDQ) to screen for child psychiatric disorders in a community sample. *International Review of Psychiatry*, *15*(1–2), 166–172.

Greenberg, M. T., Weissberg, R. P., O'Brien, M. U., Zins, J. E., Fredericks, L., Resnik, H., & Elias, M. J. (2003). Enhancing school-based prevention and youth development through coordinated social, emotional, and academic learning. *The American Psychologist*, *58*(6–7), 466.

Hadwin, J. A., Garner, M., & Perez-Olivas, G. (2006). The development of information processing biases in childhood anxiety: A review and exploration of its origins in parenting. *Clinical Psychology Review*, *26*(7), 876–894.

Halpern, L. F. (2004). The relations of coping and family environment to preschoolers' problem behavior. *Journal of Applied Developmental Psychology*, *25*(4), 399–421.

Hema, D. A., Roper, S. O., Nehring, J. W., Call, A., Mandleco, B. L., & Dyches, T. T. (2009). Daily stressors and coping responses of children and adolescents with type 1 diabetes. *Child: Care, Health and Development*, *35*, 330–339.

Holen, S., Lervåg, A., Waaktaar, T., & Ystgaard, M. (2012). Exploring the associations between coping patterns for everyday stressors and mental health in young schoolchildren. *Journal of School Psychology*, *50*(2), 167–193.

Hudson, B. L., & Buchanan, A. (2000). *Promoting children's emotional well-being: Messages from research.* Oxford; New York: Oxford University Press, c2000.

Jenkins, J. M., Smith, M. A., & Graham, P. J. (1989). Coping with parental quarrels. *Journal of the American Academy of Child and Adolescent Psychiatry*, *28*(2), 182–189.

Kagan, J. (1997). Temperament and the reactions to unfamiliarity. *Child Development*, *68*(1), 139–143.

Kagan, J., Snidman, N., Arcus, D., & Reznick, J. S. (1994). *Galen's prophecy: Temperament in human nature.* New York, NY: Basic Books.

Kerig, P. K. (2001). Children's coping with interparental conflict. In I. J. J. Grych & H. Fincham (Eds.), *Interparental conflict and child development* (pp. 213–248). New York: Cambridge University Press.

Kiernan, N., Frydenberg, E., Deans, J., & Liang, R. (2017). The relationship between parent-reported coping, stress, and mental health in a pre-school population. *Educational and Developmental Psychologist, 34*(2), 124–141.

Kohlberg, L. (1984). *Essays in moral development: Vol. 2. The psychology of moral development.* New York: Harper & Row.

Konold, T. R., Brewster, J. C., & Pianta, R. C. (2004). The behaviour of child behaviour ratings: Measurement structure of the child behaviour checklist across time, informants, and child gender. *Journal of Behavioral Disorders, 29*, 372–383.

Krohne, H. W., & Hock, M. (1991). Relationships between restrictive mother-child interactions and anxiety of the child. *Anxiety Research, 4*(2), 109–124.

Lazarus, R. S., & Folkman, S. (1984). *Stress, appraisal, and coping.* New York: Springer Publishing Company.

McClure, E. B., Brennan, P. A., Hammen, C., & Le Brocque, R. M. (2001). Parental anxiety disorders, child anxiety disorders, and the perceived parent–child relationship in an Australian high-risk sample. *Journal of Abnormal Child Psychology, 29*(1), 1–10.

Miller, K. S., Vannatta, K., Compas, B. E., Vasey, M., McGoron, K. D., Salley, C. G., & Gerhardt, C. A. (2009). The role of coping and temperament in the adjustment of children with cancer. *Journal of Pediatric Psychology, 34*, 1135–1143.

Moreland, A., & Dumas, J. (2008). Evaluating child coping competence: Theory and measurement. *Journal of Child & Family Studies, 17*(3), 437–454. doi:10.1007/s10826-007-9165-y

Morren, M., Muris, P., Kindt, M., Schouten, E., & van Den Hout, M. (2008). Emotional reasoning and parent-based reasoning in non-clinical children, and their prospective relationships with anxiety symptoms. *Child Psychiatry and Human Development, 39*(4), 351–367.

Nicolotti, L., El-Sheikh, M., & Whitson, S. M. (2003). Children's coping with marital conflict and their adjustment and physical health: Vulnerability and protective functions. *Journal of Family Psychology, 17*(3), 315–326.

O'Brien, M., Bahadur, M. A., Gee, C., Balto, K., & Erber, S. (1997). Child exposure to marital conflict and child coping responses as predictors of child adjustment. *Cognitive Therapy and Research, 21*(1), 39–59.

Pahl, K. M., Barrett, P. M., & Gullo, M. J. (2012). Examining potential risk factors for anxiety in early childhood. *Journal of Anxiety Disorder, 26*, 311–320.

Pang, I., Frydenberg, E., & Deans, J. (2015). The relationship between anxiety and coping in pre-schoolers. In P. Buchenwald & K. Moore (Eds.), *Anxiety, stress & coping* (pp. 26–27). Berlin: Verlag.

Payton, J., Weissberg, R., Durlak, J., Dymnicki, A., Taylor, R., Schellinger, K., & Pachan, M. (2008). *The positive impacts of social and emotional learning for kindergarten to eighth grade students: Findings from three scientific reviews.* Chicago, IL: CASEL.

Pincus, D. B., & Friedman, A. G. (2004). Improving children's coping with everyday stress: Transporting treatment interventions to the school setting. *Clinical Child and Family Psychology Review, 7*(4), 223–240.

Rachman, S. (1998). *Anxiety*. Hove, UK: Psychology Press.

Rapee, R. M. (2002). The development and modification of temperamental risk for anxiety disorders: Prevention of a lifetime of anxiety? *Biological Psychiatry, 52*(10), 947–957.

Rapee, R. M., Schniering, C. A., & Hudson, J. L. (2009). Anxiety disorders during childhood and adolescence: Origins and treatment. *Annual Review of Clinical Psychology, 5*, 311–341.

Rothbart, M. K. (2007). Temperament, development, and personality. *Current Directions in Psychological Science, 16*(4), 207–212. doi:10.1111/j.1467-8721.2007.00505.x

Rothbart, M. K., & Derryberry, D. (1981). Development of individual differences in temperament. In M. E. Lamb & A. Brown (Eds.), *Advances in developmental psychology* (Vol. 1, pp. 37–86). Hillsdale, NJ: Erlbaum.

Roza, S. J., Hofstra, M. B., van der Ende, J., & Verhulst, F. C. (2003). Stable prediction of mood and anxiety disorders based on behavioral and emotional problems in childhood: A 14-year follow-up during childhood, adolescence, and young adulthood. *The American Journal of Psychiatry, 160*, 2116–2121. doi:10.1176/appi.ajp.160.12.2116

Sanson, A., Pedlow, R., Cann, W., Prior, M., & Oberklaid, F. (1996). Shyness ratings: Stability and correlates in early childhood. *International Journal of Behavioral Development, 19*(4), 705–724.

Seiffge-Krenke, I. (2000). Causal links between stressful events, coping style, and adolescent symptomatology. *Journal of Adolescence, 23*, 675–691. doi:10.1006/jado.2000.0352

Skinner, E. A., & Zimmer-Gembeck, M. J. (2007). The development of coping. *Annual Review of Psychology, 58*, 119–144. doi:10.1146/annurev.psych.58.110405.085705

Skinner, E. A., & Zimmer-Gembeck, M. J. (2009). Challenges to the developmental study of coping. In E. A. Skinner & M. J. Zimmer-Gembeck (Eds.), *Coping and the development of regulation. New directions for child and adolescent development* (Vol. 124, pp. 5–17). San Francisco: Jossey-Bass. doi:10.1002/cd.239

Spence, S. H., Rapee, R., McDonald, C., & Ingram, M. (2001). The structure of anxiety symptoms among pre-schoolers. *Behaviour Research and Therapy, 39*, 1293–1316.

Suveg, C., & Zeman, J. (2004). Emotion regulation in children with anxiety disorders. *Journal of Clinical Child and Adolescent Psychology, 33*(4), 750–759.

Thompson, R. J., Mata, J., Jaeggi, S. M., Buschkuehl, M., Jonides, J., & Gotlib, I. H. (2010). Maladaptive coping, adaptive coping, and depressive symptoms: Variations across age and depressive state. *Behaviour Research and Therapy, 48*, 459–466.

Valiente, C., Lemery-Chalfant, K., & Swanson, J. (2009). Children's responses to daily social stressors: Relations with parenting, children's effortful control, and adjustment. *Journal of Child Psychology and Psychiatry, 50*(6), 707–717.

Vostanis, P. (2006). Strengths and Difficulties Questionnaire: Research and clinical applications. *Current Opinion in Psychiatry, 19*(4), 367–372.

Wadsworth, M. E., Raviv, T., Compas, B. E., & Connor-Smith, J. K. (2005). Parent and adolescent responses to poverty-related stress: Tests of mediated and moderated coping models. *Journal of Child and Family Studies, 14*(2), 283–298.

Whalen, D. J., Sylvester, C. M., & Luby, J. L. (2017). Depression and anxiety in pre-schoolers. A review of the past 7 years. *Child and Adolescent Psychiatric Clinics of North America*, 26, 503–522. doi:10.1016/j.chc.2017.02.006

Williams, K. E., & Berthelsen, D. (2017). The development of prosocial behaviour in early childhood: Contributions of early parenting and self-regulation. *International Journal of Early Childhood*, 49(1), 73–94.

Woerner, W., Fleitlich-Bilyk, B., Martinussen, R., Fletcher, J., Cucchiaro, G., Dalgalarrondo, P., ... Tannock, R. (2004). The Strengths and Difficulties Questionnaire overseas: Evaluations and applications of the SDQ beyond Europe. *European Child & Adolescent Psychiatry*, 13(2), ii47-ii54.

Wright, M., Banerjee, R., Hoek, W., Rieffe, C., & Novin, S. (2010). Depression and social anxiety in children: Differential links with coping strategies. *Journal of Abnormal Child Psychology*, 38, 405–419.

Yeo, K., Frydenberg, E., Northam, E., & Deans, J. (2014). Coping with stress among pre-school children and associations with anxiety level and controllability of situations. *Australian Journal of Psychology*, 66(2), 93–101.

Chapter 7

Teaching coping skills in the context of positive parenting

Box 7.1 A mother's reflection on their own coping practices upon completion of the *Families Coping* program

J and I have been reflecting on how much we gained from the positive parenting course over these past few weeks and wanted to write to thank you for your efforts and calm in facilitating ... our mantra has become 'we are calm and in control' in the times that we are challenged, and after the fact, we talk about what character strength that behaviour will become for our littles ones down the track. We really loved the story sharing and connect with other parents experiencing similar issues. As a bonus J has been able to take some of the positive reframing techniques into his male-dominated workplace in his ongoing efforts. (Mother participant in *Families Coping* program)

'I showed my family a sad feeling last night. I wanted them to guess it. My body was down, my eyes were sad and my mouth was down. My sister Zara asked are you Angry – I said no. Dad said you are definitely not happy and mum said you look really sad. Mum guessed my feelings because she knows how I feel when I am sad in real life.'

~ Eddie, 5-year-old

Overview

Children learn and adopt coping practices from their parents at a very young age, both through observation and subsequent imitation and through direct instruction. Such engagements between parents and their children serve to foster the development of social emotional competence in the early years. Drawing on the latest research in early years coping and parenting, this chapter provides ways to introduce families to evidence-based positive communication, collaborative problem-solving and proactive/productive coping skills to incorporate into their own parenting practices. It allows parents to reflect on their own coping practices and utilise language in the family context that both mirrors those represented in the children's visual coping tools such as the Early Years Coping Cards (see Chapter 4). There are some easy to implement strategies for parents to access from their 'parenting toolbox' so as to help raise happy, confident and respectful children. The chapter also provides examples of culturally-responsive tools for culturally and linguistically diverse (CALD) families.

Theoretical basis and research

Positive parenting and early years well-being

Positive parenting lays the foundations for well-being in the early years of life through establishing a safe, stable, engaging and nurturing environment that promotes optimal children's development (Sanders & Morawska, 2017). It is well established that the quality of parent–child interactions can play a crucial role in promoting not only positive mental health outcomes and social emotional competencies in the early years (Taylor & Biglan, 1998; Wilson, Havighurst & Harley, 2012) but can also support the growth of early language, school readiness (Bayer et al., 2011; Vassallo et al., 2002) and paves the way for long-term health and well-being as children develop into adults (Calvert & Smith, 2004; Mistry et al., 2012).

Parenting programs have been shown to be an effective way of improving children's behaviour and family well-being, particularly when delivered in a group format (Barlow et al., 2011; Furlong et al., 2012; Wilson et al., 2012). Since the 70s and 80s, there have been numerous group-based parenting programs such as the Parent Effectiveness Training (Gordon, 1970) and Systematic Training for Effective Parenting (Dinkmeyer, McKay & Dinkmeyer, 1989). The core principles which underscore these programs are good communication skills and the notion that all children's behaviour is intentional (Dreikurs, 1958). In more recent years, positive parenting offerings such as the Triple P Positive Parenting Program (Sanders, Markie-Dadds, Tully & Bor, 2000), The Incredible Years (Webster-Stratton, Jamila Reid & Stoolmiller, 2008) and Parent Management Training (Pearl, 2009) highlight the common focus of enhancing parenting skills, providing knowledge and developing positive attitudes towards parenting. Positive parenting programs are underscored by models of social learning and behavioural principles which orientate parents to consider what skills and behaviours would better serve their children and how to promote those in the family context (Mazzucchelli & Sanders, 2014). The ultimate goal of these programs is to develop the child's social and emotional competencies through addressing parent-specific variables (e.g. communication practices and parent behaviours).

Although the 21st century has brought about many changes to the wider environmental context within which parents and families operate, such as the rise of single parenthood, blended families, parenting in a world dominated by technology and social media, there are core principles of family life that remain constant in a fast-paced changing world. The ideal family is where;

- communication is positive and effective
- issues are discussed, and conflicts raised
- parents can express concerns about likely consequences.

In other words, in the ideal family parents are confident and capable of taking charge and children are nurtured with respect, love and empathy, with a focus on understanding and capitalising on the strengths of each individual when facing everyday challenges (Frydenberg, 2015; Sanders, 2008). It is comprised of members who act to construct a functional coping repertoire over time that is time- and situation-appropriate (Deans, Frydenberg & Tsurutani, 2010) (see Chapters 5 and 6 for definition and details on coping).

Building a shared language of coping: the role of parents

One key factor that contributes to both parents' and children's healthy adaptation to everyday experiences is their capacity to cope (Armstrong, Birnie-Lefcovitch & Ungar, 2005; Cooklin, Giallo & Rose, 2011). The ability of parents to manage the demands associated with raising a child, as well as show willingness to engage in a process of self-enquiry to improve their parenting practice and learn new skills, inherently calls on the use of everyday coping skills.

Parent coping and well-being

For some time, it has been clear that a prerequisite for teaching children how to cope is that it is important that adults first learn to understand their own coping and learn to use the concepts and language of coping that we want children to acquire. When seeking to improve coping, an explicit focus on descriptions of what is helpful and unhelpful coping is important as it provides a common language for understanding coping practices and provides a basis for parent reflection on their own coping behaviours. In research from a non-clinical large sample of Australian parents with children aged 5 or under, non-productive coping strategies such as self-blame and disengagement were found to be related to greater parental fatigue which in turn was linked to greater parental stress, increased irritability in parent–child communication and lower parental competence (Cooklin et al., 2011). On the other hand, an increase in parent use of productive coping strategies increases a variety of positive outcomes for parents. For example, the use of productive coping strategies such as social support, family cohesion and problem-focused coping have been linked with reduced stress and fewer depressive symptoms in parents whose children suffer from chronic health conditions (Churchill, Villareale, Monaghan, Sharp & Kieckhefer, 2010; Rodenburg, Meijer, Deković & Aldenkamp, 2007), as well as in parents of typically developing children (Dabrowski & Pisula, 2010).

Moreover, parenting styles and parent coping strategies are likely to interact with and impact positive outcomes on children's coping. Parental warmth was shown to be predictive of children's use of problem coping strategies (Wolfradt, Hempel & Miles, 2003). Children with mothers who practice authoritative parenting that is firm and clear with reasons being given for what is required, were more likely to disclose their worries and concerns, which in turn predicted the use of positive coping strategies such as seeking social support and self-reliance or problem-solving (Almas, Grusec & Tackett, 2011). Another study in the pre-school population found that the use of less productive coping by a father predicted higher levels of aggression in their sons at school (Foster, Reese-Weber & Kahn, 2007).

The main message from these studies is that parents can influence their children's coping by modelling the use of productive coping strategies. Parents are also in the best position to give insight into their children's emotional experiences and coping responses through day-to-day inter-actions and effective communications (Cassano, Perry-Parrish & Zeman, 2007; Deans, Frydenberg & Liang, 2012).

Application

Families Coping program

Building upon the transactional model of stress and coping (see Chapter 5) and drawing upon research on parent and child coping (see Chapters 5 and 6), a parenting program which included a comprehensive focus on parents' and children's coping was developed. The *Families Coping* (FC) program is a ten-hour universal social emotional parenting program within the frame-work of positive parenting. It integrates parenting skills with communica-tion skills and focuses on how healthy families with children in the early years can enhance their productive coping whilst weakening the engage-ment with non-productive coping activities. The program explicitly addresses the models of coping detailed in earlier chapters and utilises the Coping Scale for Adults (CSA; Frydenberg & Lewis, 1997 – see Chapter 5 for details) at the beginning of the program and upon completion of the program so that parents can ascertain and reflect on their own coping prac-tices, such as the example given in Box 7.1.

There are five key elements to the *Families Coping* program:

- The **first** is to contextualise parenting in a framework of positive psychological practice. The importance of self-care for parents is highlighted. Parents are made aware of how they can capitalise on positive emotions (e.g. gratitude and love) and a focus on strengths to prevent burnout. Children's strengths, like that of each of us, occur in a range of spheres. Parents are encouraged to consider their child's strengths in areas such as bravery (shows courage to take on challenges and deal with difficult situations), curiosity (likes exploring and asking questions and takes an interest in experiences), creativity (thinks of new ways to do things), enthusiasm (approaches things with excitement and energy), fairness (treating others with a sense of equality and justice), humour (likes to laugh and joke and bring smiles to other people), kindness (does things that make others happy) and sociability (is able to engage with others).
- The **second** is to examine adult coping skills: what is good coping and what is unhelpful coping. Coping practices can be changed as long as we know what to change, for what purpose and how to do it. Parents are introduced to the conceptual areas of coping, they learn to generate their own coping profile and consider their coping strengths and resources.
- **Thirdly**, there is the foundational skill of communication, reflective listening, which identifies the thoughts that are being expressed and the underlying feelings being experienced. How to respond helpfully is a learnt skill.
- The **fourth** element is the skill of taking charge as a parent and being assertive when appropriate. Parents are encouraged to consider this in the context of development, remembering that children can develop at different rates for different aspects of development (physically, emotionally and cognitively) – see developmental chart in Chapter 2 for an indication to parents as to what they can expect at what stage.
- The **fifth** skill draws on communication skills such as listening, being assertive when tackling problems and skills for collaborative problem-solving.
- The **final** element is helping children to develop skills to cope with situations that are pertinent to them at their own life stage.

The above elements are underscored by a focus on well-being and the capacity to live a good life. Mindfulness, which is the contemporary expression of being relaxed and staying in the here and now rather than dwelling on the past, is included for both parents and children as it is helpful in most circumstances where the emphasis is to stay calm and remain clear-sighted (Harnett & Dawe, 2019; Whitehead, 2011).

We also know from decades of research that the most helpful coping strategy is that of social support. Recognising when a parent needs a helping hand, someone to talk to or a place to let off steam without being judged. Most significantly, knowing where those supports are and how to access them is itself reassuring. In contrast, the least helpful coping strategy is one where parents blame themselves when things go wrong rather than learning from the experience. Self-blame is the least helpful coping strategy. Rather than being overly critical or judgemental towards themselves – as a person or as a parent – the importance of self-compassion is highlighted as it can help us to accept our own imperfections and to embrace that in others. Research has shown self-compassion helps us to better accept the present and the struggles of life with greater ease and can lead to a happier, more fulfilling life (Neff & Germer, 2017; Warren, Smeets & Neff, 2016).

Families Coping (Frydenberg, 2015) focuses on positive experiences in the family that include catching children when they are doing something well rather than when they are doing something wrong, having pleasurable family experiences, modelling appreciation and gratitude and above all knowing where to get support when parents need it. Through the teaching of communication and coping skills in the context of positive parenting the *Families Coping* program supports families to deal with circumstances that they encounter as part of their everyday lives in a productive and pro-active way (Frydenberg, Deans & Liang, 2014). It is about bringing up children who are engaged with the world around them, who retain curiosity to explore their environment and gain satisfaction when they accomplish a task. We want children not only to be willing to engage in challenging activities but also able to engage with and relate to others, to show gratitude and to appreciate their surroundings. Table 7.1 provides an overview of the key strategies covered in the *Families Coping* program.

Evidence

The *Families Coping* program has undergone evaluations in 2013 and 2014 across parent and child coping and well-being measures, as well as qualitative analysis for parents' experience throughout the program. The studies demonstrate that parents reported greater use of productive coping: improving relationships, seeking relaxing diversions and physical recreation; and a concurrent reduction in non-productive coping skills: worry, tension reduction, self-blame and keeping to self. Qualitative written responses from parents also indicated that over a third of them perceived a trend towards the development of more positive parenting practices and use of productive coping by their child, as well as some aspect of improvement in both parent and child well-being (Gulliford, Deans, Frydenberg & Liang, 2015; Thomson, Frydenberg, Deans & Liang, 2015). This is consistent with the changes observed in coping, with research showing a positive association between productive coping and well-being (Cheng, Mauno &

Table 7.1 Key strategies for parents at a glance

Setting the scene for positive parenting
- Take care of yourself physically, emotionally and socially
- Build your personal and social resources and identify support
- Identify, recognise and utilise strengths of each family member
- Make time for gratitude and taking in good experiences.

Building effective communication with your family
- Practise reflective listening to understand others' needs and concerns
- Remember that all children's behaviour is purposeful: look for the 'hidden' message
- Take charge as a parent by asserting your needs and concerns (for example use I-statements)
- Employ the collaborative problem-solving model to brainstorm creative options, consider alternatives and build win-win solutions.

Modelling productive coping as a parent
- Focus on increasing your use of productive coping strategies and reducing non-productive ones such as self-blame
- Take notice of negative thinking and reframe it positively such as 'I can't cope' → 'I can manage the situation'. Remember positive thoughts lead to positive feelings and hope
- Believe in your capacity to cope and ask for help in times of need
- Learn to manage conflict utilising skills such as assertive communication and problem-solving
- If you feel uncomfortable talking to friends or family, remember there is another option: such as seeking professional help from doctors, counsellors or psychologists who are trained to assess situations and help people to better understand and manage their responses by developing effective coping strategies – no matter how big or small the issue.

Practising mindfulness as a family
- Listen with attention, patience and curiosity
- Accept whatever your child is presenting
- Build emotional awareness of yourself and your child
- Cultivate compassion for yourself and your child
- Engage your child with daily mindfulness exercises.

Lee, 2014; Frydenberg & Lewis, 2011; Mayordomo-Rodriques, Melendez-Moral, Viguer-Segui & Sales-Galan, 2014), and a negative association between non-productive coping and well-being (Chu-Lien Chao, 2011; Gustems-Carnicer & Calderon, 2013).

Combined research data on comparison of results between gender and partner attendance groups in the *Families Coping* program showed minimal differences in program effectiveness. Overall experience has told us that when both parents attend they get onto the same page quickly. They use the parenting sessions as a way of regrouping, having some reflective time together and focusing on both their own needs and that of their children. Nevertheless, our research study has found that regardless of whether it is single parent attendance or both parents participating there are benefits (Thomson et al., 2015). Parents saw the benefits of positive parenting and became aware of their personal strengths and that of their children. Many of the benefits post program include their feeling that parents became more aware of their emotions and that of their children, they acquired new communication skills which helped to improve their connectedness with their children, coping skills for themselves and their children, an appreciation of mindful living and parenting and the importance of their own well-being as well as that of their children.

The principles embodied in the *Families Coping* program are universal in that being positive and caring for oneself as an adult, as well as caring for others, applies in most contexts where people exist together. Additionally, good communication skills such as being a good listener, being assertive rather than blaming oneself or others and utilising problem-solving skills as appropriate. The skills can readily be transferred to other settings such as where people interact. This was highlighted by the parent who is quoted at the outset of the chapter. Modelling good practices to children is important. They can also be translated into cross-cultural settings where the concepts have to be communicated clearly and effectively. This approach was taken with a group of culturally and linguistically diverse families.

Parenting support for CALD families

The early years provide a window of opportunity to engage parents in mental health promotion and the development of healthy parent–child relationships which support well-being in childhood and over the life course. This is of particular relevance for families with young children from culturally and linguistically diverse (CALD) backgrounds and disadvantaged communities, who may be more vulnerable to experiencing multiple and complex life problems and hence benefit from community resources that support their everyday needs, in particular their parenting (Sandler, Ingram, Wolchik, Tein & Winslow, 2015).

Contextualising program to fit the needs of parents in CALD and disadvantaged communities

Families with young children from CALD and disadvantaged backgrounds (e.g. poverty) are disproportionately exposed to family and neighbourhood-level risk factors (e.g. low maternal education and/or low parental income) that can place them at risk for accumulated stress (Parker, 2009) and adverse outcomes such as emotional difficulties and peer problems

(Mullainathan & Shafir, 2013; Priest, Baxter & Hayes, 2012). Effective and accessible services that support the use of positive and productive parenting practices can be a promising focus for early intervention and prevention for these families through training and education.

The early years productive parenting program

Contextual influences are important for guaranteeing a successful uptake of services on offer to parents (Bronfenbrenner, 1979; Kelly, 2006). Thus building on the *Families Coping* program, an inclusive model of a community-based parenting program titled the *Early Years Productive Parenting Program* (EYPPP) was developed and piloted over five weeks in a council community playgroup in a housing-estate located in inner-city Melbourne, Australia (Frydenberg, Deans & Liang, 2017). It is important to embed services in the natural settings of these families whilst increasing flexibility of the offerings to align with the goals and needs of those settings, that is, a community and family-centred approach to improve the reach and engagement of program offerings at a community level for disadvantaged families (Lakind & Atkins, 2018). The playgroup setting was one in which families from CALD backgrounds meet regularly to make friends, share ideas and experiences in raising children and also to facilitate their child's play with other children (Figure 7.1). A model of flexible delivery was implemented to enable adaptation to the individual needs of families and integrated into existing community playgroup activities (e.g. informal conversations infused with core parenting principles). Also, with the support of the playgroup centre staff, facilitators of the EYPPP were able to have more in-depth conversations with parents and work in a culturally-appropriate way.

Within this context the EYPPP was delivered to support parents to ensure that they could draw on a range of universal and culturally-appropriate tools and resources (such as sets of culturally-sensitive Early Years Coping Cards that are described in Chapter 4) and a set of image-based simple text 'Parenting Tip Sheets' to communicate effectively and develop warm and trusting relationships with their children and in so doing help their children to gain a greater sense of self and overall well-being. Weekly session times were allotted for parents to focus discussion on skills and concerns they determined to be most immediately relevant for them.

For each session, parents were encouraged to implement the introduced tips and strategies at home (see Table 7.2) and to provide feedback during the following session (see Figure 7.2 for an example). All participating families were provided with a 'Parenting Tips' booklet containing all the key messages from the sessions as a resource that they could draw upon in their everyday parenting journey into the future.

Figure 7.1 Conducting the EYPPP in a council community playgroup setting

Evidence

The EYPPP helps parents align their cultural practices with those of the local community, in this case the Australian context, while at the same time endorsing the individual family's cultural practices, languages and identity. Throughout the five sessions, parents learnt how to incorporate the practice of positive, practical coping strategies into their own parenting practice and also how they could involve their children in developmentally appropriate activities to enrich their development (Scerra, 2010).

Program evaluation data (Deans, Liang & Frydenberg, 2016) suggests that a flexible-delivery parenting program such as the EYPPP has the potential to strengthen productive coping capacities in families and in doing so contribute to the overall well-being of young children. The EYPPP is accessible for parents of both genders. However, from the experience of the leaders in this project, it is usually the mothers who sign up for these programs to gain skills and support in their parenting journey. It is also most frequently reported by mothers that they find these initiatives helpful. Quoting one mother of Sudanese background who provided feedback to a small pilot trial of playgroup-based parents engagement program in 2013: 'When I try to use soft voice (one of the

Table 7.2 Simplified parenting tips for CALD families (especially for under-5s)

Supporting health and well-being in a family context with young children
- Catch your child doing something good
- Take time out for my own well-being
- Praise effort
- Celebrate good behaviour
- Build a support network
- Use distraction strategies when needed.

Parents dealing with difficult situations
- Use a soft voice for discipline and a loud voice for having fun
- Use kind words with each other in the family
- Use 3 Ss with my child 'See, Show, Say'
- Teach child: 'Don't go for a yes when you already have a no'.

Listening to children and understanding behaviour
- Talk to your child – use I-messages[1]
- Read to your child
- Play with your child
- Plan against boredom.

Collaborative problem-solving with young children
- Set simple family rules
- Have clear limits
- Enforce family rules consistently
- Remember every problem has a solution.

Mindfulness in the family
- Keep calm and maintain a sense of humour
- Establish opportunities for quiet activity
- Practise finding the time and space for oneself
- Create quality time together.

parenting tips offered during the program) not only with my son but also my husband, he starts saying nice things back to me ... and I feel good about that ... ' It demonstrates and highlights the crucial role of mothers in building a healthy family environment for their young children and the value of such initiatives particularly for families from the CALD and/or disadvantaged backgrounds. Below is a summary of the new knowledge learnt identified by the EYPPP participants (see Table 7.3).

---

1 I-message is a form of assertive communication that enables the concerned person, generally the parent, to be assertive, to declare his or her need or needs while at the same time respecting the other. E.g. Rather than 'Can't you hurry up, you will be late for school again!', 'I need us to be out of the house by seven o'clock in the morning so that we can get to school on time and I can get to work.'

IV. Collaborative problem-solving with young children

❖ Set simple family rules *(e.g. establish rules based on what is important in my family–safety?)*

❖ Have clear limits *(e.g. make it clear & understood what is okay to do –when & where children play, who they play with, and when it is time to stop.)*

❖ Show by example *(e.g. show my child how to care for books by carefully turning the pages when reading together.)*

❖ Enforce family rules consistently *(e.g. when it is bath time/bed time, sit down to eat, be gentle with each other.)*

❖ Remember every problem has a solution *(e.g. working with my partner or child using the six steps of problem solving–Define problem → Brainstorm solutions → Evaluate solutions → Choose solutions → Plan & Take action → Check Results to sort out a problem.)*

Notes to myself...

"Hard to get all of my six kids to eat dinner at the same time...they learnt that no dinner for them if they don't come during dinner time."

"When I try to use soft voice with my husband, he starts saying nice things back to me.... and I feel good about that..."

Figure 7.2 An example on how parents utilised the weekly Parenting Tip Sheet for reflection

Two elements in the delivery of EYPPP were identified as most valuable to parents: a) topics were revisited over multiple sessions to build parental skills and confidence over time; b) one-on-one (researcher/facilitator and parent) conversations in the playgroup's natural setting also allowed for deeper understanding of concerns of each individual family, and for facilitators to address those needs promptly and sensitively. The inclusion of the 'voices of parents' in community-based parenting programs such as the EYPPP program can affirm and expand parents' confidence to address the challenges faced during the everyday parenting journey and to share their experiences with others (e.g. a new mother mentioned: 'I learnt a lot from other parents – especially the one with five children. Back in Africa it is so hard, with no opportunities etc. This is a good opportunity to learn and talk.'), thereby building community support beyond the program duration.

Understandably, how people benefit from such experiences varies according to their needs and the settings in which such programs are delivered. A no-cost, easy-to-access program provides a unique opportunity for parents to feel at ease in a familiar setting and take the first steps to incorporate evidence-based parenting practices into their lives, echoing what research has confirmed about the value of prevention and early intervention programs for vulnerable families.

Table 7.3 New knowledge learnt from each of the five sessions of EYPPP

Session	New Knowledge
1. Focusing on well-being	• 'I go to my parents or friends when I feel stressed.' • 'I take time to go for a walk with my children at the nearest park when I can't handle the stress at home.' • 'Better ways to discipline and reward behaviour.' • 'Think of when to reward my child.'
2. Learning new ways to deal with challenging situations	• 'I am still learning how to do the soft voice for discipline because it is hard to change the habit.' • 'It's like changing from automatic mode to manual mode – reminding myself to use soft voice.' • 'Three Ss – See, Show, Say and repeating words.' • 'Things to look out for and ways to deal with them.'
3. Communicating with children	• 'We talk all the time, always look for alternatives before I explode … ' • 'I am busy then … but I told my child we can talk later … ' • 'Ways to communicate to make things easier and calmer.' • 'Try listen even though I have different age groups.'
4. Problem-solving	• 'Hard to get all of my six kids to eat dinner at the same time … they learnt that no dinner for them if they don't come during dinner time.' • 'When I try to use soft voice with my husband, he starts saying nice things back to me … and I feel good about that … ' • 'I learnt to use a soft voice.'
5. Mindfulness in the family	• 'Slowly knocking off [bad] habits – one at a time and be conscious about it.' • 'Changing from stress talk to health talk is not an easy job, it is very difficult, but when everyday using [it and try to] remember what I've learnt, it works … by saying I can do this thing … ' • 'Enjoy the moment.' • 'Children need me and not just money.'

A flexible model can be adapted to a range of settings to increase levels of awareness in the CALD or disadvantaged communities of the importance of effective parenting as a means for modelling and building social and emotional competence in young children and hence improving their well-being over time.

Summary remarks

The core elements that we have deemed desirable in a parenting program include communication skills, adult and child coping skills and a focus on self-care for the parent. A universal parenting program that is in an accessible, readable format with activities for a parent to complete is able to be used in numerous ways. For example,

- The contents can be offered to parents to help them reflect on their parenting practices in a self-help or group setting.
- If only one parent is able to attend the other parent has the benefit of the contents either verbally if shared by the attending partner or in written form.
- The program can be offered by a group leader or in combination with the person engaged with the child in an early learning setting.
- If a parent group is conducted parents have the benefit of recognising that they are not alone in finding parenting to be challenging.
- Like-minded parent participants can often become a support group for each other.
- A parenting program that has text along with activities can be offered for distance education for parents who are not able to attend.
- A universal parenting program based on sound principles can be adapted for a linguistically diverse population.

Take home messages

- Children learn and adopt coping practices from their parents at a very young age.
- Quality parent–child interactions can promote well-being and social emotional competencies in the early years.
- Aim to increase your use of productive coping strategies such as healthy self-talk 'I can manage, I am in charge', building social support networks and developing effective communication and problem-solving skills etc.
- Decrease your use of non-productive coping strategies such as self-blame and worry.
- Build emotional awareness of and cultivate compassion for yourself and your child.
- Celebrate good behaviour and use kind words with each other in the family.

References

Almas, A., Grusec, J. E., & Tackett, J. L. (2011). Children's disclosure and secrecy: Links to maternal parenting characteristics and children's coping skills. *Social Development, 20*(3), 624–643.

Armstrong, M. A., Birnie-Lefcovitch, S., & Ungar, M. T. (2005). Pathways between social support, family wellbeing, quality of parenting, and child resilience: What we know. *Journal of Child and Family Studies, 14,* 269–281. doi:10.1007/s10826-005-5054-4

Barlow, J., Smailagic, N., Bennett, C., Huband, N., Jones, H., & Coren, E. (2011). Individual and group based parenting programmes for improving psychosocial outcomes for teenage parents and their children. *Cochrane Database of Systematic Reviews, 2011*(3), CD002964. doi:10.1002/14651858.CD002964

Bayer, J. K., Rapee, R. M., Hiscock, H., Ukomunne, O. C., Mihalopoulos, C., Clifford, S., & Wake, M. (2011). The cool little kids randomised controlled trial: Population-level entry prevention for anxiety disorders. *Public Health, 11,* 1–9. doi:10.1186/1471-2458-11-11

Bronfenbrenner, U. (1979). Contexts of child rearing: Problems and prospects. *American Psychologist, 34,* 844–850.

Calvert, G., & Smith, R. (2004). A national framework for promoting health and well-being in the early years. *Health Promotion Journal of Australia, 15*(2), 99–102.

Cassano, M., Perry-Parrish, C., & Zeman, J. (2007). Influence of gender on parental socialization of children's sadness regulation. *Social Development, 16,* 210–231.

Cheng, T., Mauno, S., & Lee, C. (2014). Do job control, support, and optimism help job insecure employees? A three-wave study of buffering effects on job satisfaction, vigor and work–family enrichment. *Social Indicators Research, 118* (3), 1269–1291.

Chu-Lien Chao, R. (2011). Managing stress and maintaining well-being: Social support, problem-focused coping, and avoidant coping. *Journal of Counseling & Development, 89*(3), 338–348.

Churchill, S. S., Villareale, N. L., Monaghan, T. A., Sharp, V. L., & Kieckhefer, G. M. (2010). Parents of children with special health care needs who have better coping skills have fewer depressive symptoms. *Maternal Child Health Journal, 14,* 47–57. doi:10.1007/s10995-008-0435-0

Cooklin, A. R., Giallo, R., & Rose, N. (2011). Parental fatigue and parenting practices during early childhood: An Australian community survey. *Child: Care, Health and Development, 38,* 654–664. doi:10.1111/j.1365-2214.2011.01333.x

Dabrowski, A., & Pisula, E. (2010). Parenting stress and coping styles in mothers and fathers of pre-school children with autism and Down syndrome. *Journal of Intellectual Disability Research, 54,* 266–280. doi:10.1111/j.1365-2788.2010.01258.x

Deans, J., Frydenberg, E., & Liang, R. (2012). Building a shared language of coping: Dynamics of communication between parents and pre-school children. *New Zealand Research into Early Childhood Research Journal, 15,* 67–89.

Deans, J., Frydenberg, E., & Tsurutani, H. (2010). Operationalising social and emotional coping competencies in kindergarten children. *New Zealand Research In Early Childhood Education, 13,* 113–124.

Deans, J., Liang, R., & Frydenberg, E. (2016, March 1). Giving voices and providing skills to families in culturally and linguistically diverse communities through a productive parenting program. *Australasian Journal of Early Childhood, 41,* 13–18.

Dinkmeyer, D. C., McKay, G. D., & Dinkmeyer, J. S. (1989). *Parenting young children: Helpful strategies based on Systematic Training for Effective Parenting (STEP) for parents of children under six.* Circle Pines, MN: AGS.

Dreikurs, R. (1958). *The challenge of parenthood*. New York: Duell, Soan and Pearce.

Foster, P. A., Reese-Weber, M., & Kahn, J. H. (2007). Fathers' parenting hassles and coping: Associations with emotional expressiveness and their sons' socioemotional competence. *Infant and Child Development*, 16, 277–293.

Frydenberg, E. (2015). *Families Coping: Effective strategies for you and your child*. Melbourne: Australian Council for Educational Research (ACER) Press.

Frydenberg, E., Deans, J., & Liang, R. (2014). Families can do coping: Parenting skills in the early years. *Children Australia*, 39, 99–106. doi:10.1017/cha.2014.7

Frydenberg, E., Deans, J., & Liang, R. (2017). Parents and children's coping: Building resilience and wellbeing in the early years. *Social Indicators Research*. doi:10.1007/s11205-017-1752-8

Frydenberg, E., & Lewis, R. (1997). *Coping Scale for Adults*. Melbourne: Australian Council for Educational Research.

Frydenberg, E., & Lewis, R. (2011). *Adolescent Coping Scale-2*. Melbourne: Australian Council for Educational Research.

Furlong, M., McGilloway, S., Bywater, T., Hutchings, J., Smith, S. M., & Donnelly, M. (2012). Behavioural and cognitive-behavioural group-based parenting programmes for early-onset conduct problems in children aged 3 to 12 years. *Cochrane Database of Systematic Reviews*, 2012(2), CD008225. doi:10.1002/14651858.CD008225.pub2

Gordon, T. (1970). *P.E.T. Parent Effectiveness Training: The tested new way to raise responsible children*. New York: David McKay.

Gulliford, H., Deans, J., Frydenberg, E., & Liang, R. (2015). Teaching coping skills in the context of positive parenting within a pre-school setting. *Australian Psychologist*, (3), 219. doi:10.1111/ap.12121

Gustems-Carnicer, J., & Calderon, C. (2013). Coping strategies and psychological well-being among teacher education students: Coping and well-being in students. *European Journal of Psychology of Education*, 28, 1127–1140.

Harnett, P. H., & Dawe, S. (2019). The contribution of mindfulness-based therapies for children and families and proposed conceptual integration. *Child and Adolescent Mental Health*, 17(4), 195–208. doi:10.1111/j.1475-3588.2011.00643.x

Kelly, J. G. (2006). *Becoming ecological: An expedition into community psychology*. New York, NY: Oxford University Press.

Lakind, D., & Atkins, M. S. (2018). Promoting positive parenting for families in poverty: New directions for improved reach and engagement. *Children & Youth Services Review*, 89, 34–42. doi:10.1016/j.childyouth.2018.04.019

Mayordomo-Rodriques, T., Melendez-Moral, J. C., Viguer-Segui, P., & Sales-Galan, A. (2014). Coping strategies as predictors of well-being in youth adult. *Social Indicators Research*, 122(2), 479–489.

Mazzucchelli, T., & Sanders, M. (2014). Parenting from the outside-in: A paradigm shift in parent training? *Behaviour Change*, 31(2). doi:10.1017/bec.2014.4

Mistry, K. B., Minkovitz, C. S., Riley, A. W., Johnson, S. B., Grason, H. A., Dubay, L. C., & Guyer, B. (2012). A new framework for childhood health promotion: The role of policies and programs in building capacity and foundations of early childhood health. *American Journal of Public Health*, 102, 1688–1696. doi:10.2105/AJPH.2012.300687

Mullainathan, S., & Shafir, S. (2013). *Scarcity: Why having too little means so much.* New York: Times Books, Henry Holt and Company.

Neff, K. D., & Germer, C. (2017). Self-compassion and psychological wellbeing. In J. Doty (Ed.), *Oxford handbook of compassion science*, Ch. 27 (pp. 371–386). New York, NY: Oxford University Press.

Parker, R. (2009). Helping families with complex needs: Integration of the Strength to Strength and Resources for Adolescents and Parents programs. *Family Relationships Quarterly, 14*, 18–20. Retrieved 12 September 2015 from www.aifs.gov.au/afrc/pubs/newsletter/n14pdf/n14f.pdf

Pearl, E. S. (2009). Parent management training for reducing oppositional and aggressive behavior in pre-schoolers. *Aggression and Violent Behavior, 14*, 295–305. doi:10.1016/j.avb.2009.03.007

Priest, N., Baxter, J., & Hayes, L. (2012). Social and emotional outcomes of Australian children from Indigenous and culturally and linguistically diverse backgrounds. *Australian and New Zealand Journal of Public Health, 36*(2), 183–190. doi:10.1111/j.1753-6405.2011.00803.x

Rodenburg, R., Meijer, A. M., Deković, M., & Aldenkamp, A. (2007). Parents of children with enduring epilepsy: Predictors of parenting stress and parenting. *Epilepsy & Behavior, 11*, 197–207. doi:10.1016/j.yebeh.2007.05.001

Sanders, M., Markie-Dadds, C., Tully, L., & Bor, W. (2000). The Triple P – Positive Parenting Program: A comparison of enhanced, standard, and self-directed behavioral family intervention for parents of children with early onset conduct problems. *Journal of Consulting and Clinical Psychology, 68*, 624–640. doi:10.1037OT022–006X.68A624

Sanders, M. R. (2008). Triple P – Positive Parenting Program as a public health approach to strengthening parenting. *Journal of Family Psychology, 22*(3), 506–517.

Sanders, M. R., & Morawska, A. (2017). Towards an evidence-based population approach to support parenting in the early years. In P. Leach (Eds.), *Transforming infant wellbeing: Research, policy and practice for the first 1,001 critical days* (pp. 163–174). London: Taylor and Francis, c2017.

Sandler, I., Ingram, A., Wolchik, S., Tein, J., & Winslow, E. (2015). Long-term effects of parenting-focused preventive interventions to promote resilience of children and adolescents. *Child Development Perspectives, 9*(3), 164–171. doi:10. 1111/cdep.12126

Scerra, N. (2010). Effective practice in family support services: A literature review. *Developing Practice: The Child, Youth and Family Work Journal, 27*, 19.

Taylor, T. K., & Biglan, A. (1998). Behavioral family interventions for improving child-rearing: A review of the literature for clinicians and policy makers. *Clinical Child and Family Psychology Review, 1*, 41–60. doi:10.1023/A:1021848315541

Thomson, S., Frydenberg, E., Deans, J., & Liang, R. (2015). Increasing wellbeing through a parenting program: Role of gender and partnered attendance. *Australian Educational and Developmental Psychologist, 32*(2), 120–141.

Vassallo, S., Smart, D., Sanson, A., Dussuyer, I., McKendry, B., Toumbourou, J., … Oberklaid, F. (2002). *Patterns and precursors of adolescent antisocial behaviour.* First report, Crime Prevention Victoria, Department of Justice and Australian Institute of Family Studies.

Warren, R., Smeets, E., & Neff, K. D. (2016). Self-criticism and self-compassion: Risk and resilience for psychopathology. *Current Psychiatry, 15*(12), 18–32.

Webster-Stratton, C., Jamila Reid, M., & Stoolmiller, M. (2008). Preventing conduct problems and improving school readiness: Evaluation of the Incredible Years teacher and child training programs in high-risk schools. *Journal of Child Psychology and Psychiatry, 49*, 471–488. doi:10.1111/j.1469-7610.2007.01861.x

Whitehead, A. (2011). Mindfulness in early childhood education: A position paper. *Early Education, 49*, 21.

Wilson, K. R., Havighurst, S. S., & Harley, A. N. (2012). Tuning in to kids: An effectiveness trial of a parenting program targeting emotion socialisation of pre-schoolers. *Journal of Family Psychology, 26*, 56–65. doi:10.1037/a0026480

Wolfradt, U., Hempel, S., & Miles, J. N. V. (2003). Perceived parenting styles, depersonalisation, anxiety and coping behaviour in adolescents. *Personality and Individual Differences, 34*, 521–532.

Chapter 8

Approaches to pre-school Social Emotional Learning

Targeting empathy, resilience, prosocial and problem behaviour through coping strategies

'I find silence in my bedroom. Drawing makes me feel calm, especially when I draw flowers.'

~ Kevin, 4-year-old

Overview

Social Emotional Learning programs targeted at enhancing social emotional competencies and prosocial skills have the ability to promote positive development in children. This chapter features an early years social emotional program, COPE-Resilience, which incorporates the early years visual coping tools along with age-appropriate activities to enhance children's knowledge and understanding of feelings, and to learn how to care for others, communicate openly, behave in a polite and respectful manner and empathise and share with others. It explores how nurturing these skills is important for positive developmental outcomes and the vital role of educators to enable participating children to give voice to a range of social and emotional issues so that children can have the best start in life to create a better future.

Introduction

Children who demonstrate a capacity for comprehending the emotions of self and others are in general perceived as more empathic, adaptive and socially oriented. This chapter introduces the COPE-R Social Emotional Learning program in action, focusing on the role of the teacher in supporting children's development of social emotional understandings, particularly around caring and empathy. The program was delivered by a highly experienced registered early childhood teacher working with a group of twenty children aged 4 to 5 years. Underpinning the delivery was the understanding that children grow and learn in a social world where they are motivated to actively construct knowledge with peers and teachers.

Also, the program was informed by humanist theories which acknowledge the importance of relationships with others and a sense of belonging.

Teaching for social emotional competency

Over recent years there has been a growing interest in the recognition of the importance of helping young children to understand their own emotions and the emotions of others. Recent research (Belacchi & Farina, 2012; Parker, Mathis & Kupersmidt, 2013) has identified that children who demonstrate a capacity for comprehending the emotions of self and others are in general perceived as more empathic, adaptive and socially oriented. Mortari (2011) acknowledges the significance of the development of social emotional competency for all people, noting that young children are 'capable of recognizing the emotions in other subjects, revealing themselves capable of empathy' (p. 345). Also, a growing body of evidence highlights the importance of social and emotional skill development alongside academic skills for success in school and beyond (Durlak, Weissberg, Dymnicki, Taylor & Schellinger, 2011; Paulus et al., 2015).

The creation of learning environments that engage children with the processes and experiences of learning more about self and others and what it means to belong to a group are the fundamentals of the work of early years teachers. Children are supported to develop self-confidence, trust in others and learn to interact with peers with care, empathy and respect through ongoing facilitation and scaffolding by teachers. Early years curricula documents, such as The Early Years Learning Framework: Belonging, Being & Becoming (DEEWR, 2009), The Victorian Early Years Learning and Development Framework (DEECD, 2009) and Te Whāriki (NZ, Ministry of Education, 1996) each prioritise social and emotional skill development as it is recognised that it is foundational to children's social well-being and personal empowerment. A well-developed concept of self and the capacity for individuals to interact positively with others in a group are considered to be central to the learning and development of young children. As such, programs that support children's knowledge about themselves and how they fit into the community and how through the development of social emotional skills young children develop the confidence to direct his or her own learning, make an important contribution to the early years curriculum.

Social Emotional Learning (SEL) programs targeted at enhancing pro-social skills in pre-school aged children have the ability to promote positive developmental outcomes, such as a strong sense of identity, positive peer relationships, reduction in externalising problems such as physical aggression and enhanced emotional regulation (Carreras et al., 2014; Flook, Goldberg, Pinger & Davidson, 2015) and effective communication skills (DEEWR, 2009). SEL programs incorporate foundation skills such as understanding emotions in oneself and others; caring for oneself and others and learning to be a good listener and a good communicator (Durlak et al., 2011). When children can express healthy emotions, regulate them and understand the emotions of self and others, they are likely to enjoy a successful pre-school experience and demonstrate empathic capacity (Bassett, Denham & Zinsser, 2012). Empathy is described as individuals being able to understand and interpret the behaviour of others, anticipate what someone else might do and feel what others are feeling and then respond to them (Allison, Baron-Cohen, Wheelwright, Stone & Muncer, 2011). The establishment of empathetic behaviours is considered to be important for moral reasoning and overall prosocial behaviour (Decety, 2011; Feshbach & Feshbach, 2009). Baron-Cohen and Wheelwright (2004) distinguish the cognitive from the emotional dimension of empathy. While cognitive empathy comprises emotion recognition and perspective taking, emotional empathy includes phenomena of shared feelings more adequately to another person's situation than to one's own, including being able to identify and appreciate the perspective of other people. Emotional empathy development is complete in the pre-school years whereas cognitive empathy develops well into school years (Schwenck et al., 2014).

Children (4 to 7 years of age) are not only competent thinkers and communicators about their own emotions and the emotions of others, but they also have the capacity for deep reflection and develop complex arguments around emotions when given conversational prompters and guided by more competent partners (Mortari, 2011). Research has demonstrated that children can learn helpful coping skills through modelling by adults, and interactions with adults and children (Frydenberg & Deans, 2011). This can be achieved through direct teaching and the use of visual tools (e.g. the Early Years Coping Cards, Frydenberg & Deans, 2011), role-plays and games that depict issues of concern to children and how they might deal with them. As noted by Bandura (1969) the key concept in social motivation is modelling and such behaviour occurs throughout life, although the specific models change. The young infant imitates movements, facial gestures and sounds, and this modelling continues throughout the early childhood years when children model observed behaviours exhibited by parents, peers and teachers. Children model what they see and what they hear because they want to be viewed favourably in the eyes of others, therefore it is not surprising that effective SEL programs include emphasis on the role of the teacher in modelling positive communication and collaborative learning.

In addition to the content and tools that constitute an SEL program in a pre-school setting being important, a less discussed topic in this arena is the paramount role of teachers and their embodiment of the content and tools throughout the process of implementation. The connection between the teachers' embodiment of SEL, effective socialisation and implementation of SEL curriculum, and evolvement of social and emotional competence of young children is strong (Burdelski, 2010; Dachyshyn, 2015; Rosenthal & Gatt, 2010). Moreover, the stability and security of the educator (adult) learner (child) relationship directly influences SEL (DeMeulenaere, 2015; Eisenberg, Cumberland & Spinrad, 1998; Havighurst, Wilson, Harle, Prior & Kehoe, 2010). The teacher plays a pivotal role in enhancing SEL skills in children by creating a safe environment for cultivating and expressing emotions; modelling and developing empathic behaviours, encouraging and facilitating productive coping, problem-solving skills; shaping effective communication behaviours through positive reinforcement; and most importantly, weaving SEL into the school day and embodying SEL concepts moment-by-moment (Caselman, 2007; Miyamoto, Huerta & Kubacka, 2015; Rafaila, 2015). There are significant SEL gains when an experienced teacher facilitates the implementation of a purposefully designed program (Wu, Alexander, Frydenberg & Deans, 2019). As noted by Brackett, Rivers, Reyes and Salovey (2012), 'high quality' teachers led to higher student outcomes on a wide range of social and emotional variables.

The COPE-R program

The COPE-R program comprises five sessions that emphasise Care, Open-communication, Politeness, Empathy and Review; skills that support the development of critical thinking, resilience and overall individual and group well-being. The content embedded in the program aims to foster social emotional awareness and competencies that stand children in good stead in preparedness as they move into the school years (see Table 8.1 for an overview of COPE-R). Denham and Burton (2003) note that teaching social emotional competence contributes to a more sophisticated level of social emotional understanding and as such the COPE-R program could be viewed as an effective intervention program that links social emotional experiences within the family with the pre-school. As noted by Denham (1998) the three main mechanisms describe the socialisation process: modelling emotional expressiveness, teaching about emotion and reactions to children's emotions. Each of these mechanisms are understood to have a major influence on young children's overall social functioning, including the capacity of the individual to express emotion, independently self-regulate and to develop harmonious relationships with others. When provided with appropriate social emotional language the child learns to regulate emotions by attaching a label to feelings inside and bringing them to consciousness. The recognition and naming of feelings also supports the development of empathy for others (Denham & Burton, 2003).

The COPE-R program can be delivered in both small and large group learning situations over a five-week period with approximately 45 minutes dedicated to each session. It can be integrated into mainstream curricula

Table 8.1 The COPE-R program

COPE-R Session Topic	Activities
Session 1: CARING FOR OTHERS	Early Years Situation Card: Getting Hurt and Looking after someone Feelings Detective: What Is Caring? Introduce the Feelings Detective: How Are You Feeling? Pleasant/Unpleasant Feelings Language: Identify Feeling Words and Caring Behaviours Language: Caring Words to create a caring poem CARE, RESPECT, HAPPY, SAD, RELAXED, ANXIOUS Craft: Handmade Gifts for Each Other Visual Graphic: Drawing Caring Gesture: Looking After Ourselves Too Music: 'You are my Sunshine'
Session 2: OPEN- COMMUNICATION	Early Years Situation Card: Wanting to Play with Others Feelings Detective: How a Good Listener Listens Role-Play: Supportive Statements Drama: Silence & Busyness, Role-Play feelings like HAPPY, SAD, ANGRY, SURPRISED, FRUSTRATED Movement: Dancing to 3 different types of music
Session 3: POLITENESS	Early Years Situation Card: Bullied Feelings Detective: Beautiful Behaviours Feelings Detective: I'm Happy to Help Feelings Detective: Cultural Differences Role-Play: Polite Behaviours Visual Graphic: Friendly Cards and Thank You Bucket Filling: PLEASE, EXCUSE ME, THANKYOU, ARE YOU HAVING A NICE DAY? THANKYOU FOR SHARING
Session 4: EMPATHY	Early Years Situation Card: Choosing a Group to Play With. Feelings Detective: It Feels Good To Share! Feelings Detective: How Can We Share? Role-Play: Tricky Sharing Situations Art: Sharing Limited Resources Visual Graphic: We Share A Life
Session 5: REVIEW	Feelings Detective: The Caring Tree Feelings Detective: Kind Acts Role-Play: Sharing From One Tea Pot Art: Hunting and Gathering for Pleasant Feelings Art: Sending Caring Messages Around the World Art: COPE Wisdoms Game Movement: Creating a Mandala of Silence

responding to 'threads of thinking' (Nutbrown, 2011) or 'big ideas' (Perkins, 2014) established in the classroom and it can also incorporate individual or group interests as they arise. As noted, the main aim of the program is to focus on Social Emotional Learning and the role individual children play to ensure connectedness to self and the community as well as contributing to the common good of the group. Such an approach resonates with Rogoff's (1994) idea of a 'community of learners', which can be defined as a group of people who share ideas and support each other in their collective and individual learning. This brings into play the notion of establishing communal values and beliefs and recognising the importance of collaborative learning – children learning from teachers, teachers learning from children and children learning from children.

The program is also designed to provide children with opportunities for multimodal learning, which can be defined as learning that is presented in more than one sensory mode, for example visual, oral, aural, written or through the body. Such an approach is noted for its capacity to support higher quality learner outcomes (Chen & Fu, 2003; Mayer, 2003; Moreno & Mayer, 2007) especially in relation to supporting children to engage in authentic meaning-making in their immediate life worlds. As noted, the program integrates a number of meaning-making processes that include linguistic meaning making (developing a shared social emotional language), visual meaning making, audio meaning making, gestural meaning making, visual graphic meaning making and spatial meaning making. Together these modes provide access to different ways of experiencing and understanding what many consider to be abstract concepts. They are noted to promote learning by providing multiple ways of processing information and gaining learner attention by making the information more child-focused, attractive and motivating (Shah & Freedman, 2003). Interestingly, Fadel (2008) found that, 'students engaged in learning that incorporates multimodal designs, on average, outperform students who learn using traditional approaches with single modes' (p. 13).

Researching the implementation of the COPE-R program

Research indicates that it is imperative that teachers foster the development of social emotional competencies in young children and when programs purposefully target learning in these areas children are better prepared to manage their relationship building and the challenges faced in everyday life. As emotional competence is intimately related to social competence, and in turn positive well-being and good mental health, the importance of teaching skills and understandings can be seen as an effective prevention program.

As noted earlier, the COPE-R program was framed within the idea of 'community of learners' (Rogoff, 1994), which describes the active and meaningful participation of teachers and children in the learning process where the three-foci involvement of intrapersonal, interpersonal and cultural-historical-institutional influences work together to support learning. The COPE-R program was shaped to ensure collaborative participation in shared experiences where each child's contribution was valued for the knowledge, skills and experiences brought to the learning activity. By focusing on the dispositional elements of the program content the children and the teacher worked together to share their knowledge, understandings, skills and feelings, motivate and support each other and develop respect and responsibility in their relationships (Rogoff, 1998).

The research that investigated the COPE-R program aimed to investigate the nature of the program and the role of the teacher in facilitating children's social emotional learning. The research was firmly grounded in the qualitative interpretative realm and importantly it was framed in such a way to ensure that the children's voices were centrally located in the study (Jans, 2004; Page, 2007; Piscetelli & McArdle, 1999; Roberts, 2000). A case study approach was taken to allow a holistic examination of the lived experience (van Manen, 1990) of the children's Social Emotional Learning program and the role of the teacher in designing, implementing and evaluating the program.

Thirty-eight 4- and 5-year-old children and their teacher from an inner-city long-day kindergarten program participated in the research. The teacher was highly qualified and experienced and committed to the implementation of the COPE-R program as part of her mainstream program. Ethics approval was granted by the Human Ethics Research Committee, at the University where the study was undertaken (ERC Project No is 1,135,950) prior to the commencement of the research.

The data included expansive teacher-researchers' program plans and reflective journal notes, children's drawing-tellings and learning products, transcribed child interview data and photographs (Wright, 2007a; 2007b). An inductive analytical approach was taken for the examination of the data (Merriman & Guerin, 2006; Moustakas, 1994) with the analysis involving firstly a broad sweep of the entire collection, the aim being to uncover the main categories and themes that were represented across the entire sample. Secondly, the content analysis was undertaken of individual child drawing-tellings with a view to identifying how individual children used graphic representations and narratives to explain their social emotional understandings.

What the research revealed

The analysis of data highlighted the social emotional capacities of the children throughout the course of the COPE-R program especially in relation to:

- giving voice to social emotional issues,
- enacting relational empathy,
- demonstrating care for others and the environment and recognising emotions in self and others.

Giving voice to emotional issues

The teacher supported the children to identify a wide range of words to describe feeling states, for example: 'GOOD FEELINGS that make our bodies happy and relaxed'. The vocabulary was varied and described both 'GOOD' and 'BAD FEELINGS', 'HARD FEELINGS and PLEASANT and UNPLEASANT FEELINGS that make our body hard or shaky and jelly-fish like'. The children also used colloquial and imaginative metaphorical language to describe feelings, for example, going bananas, being bored out of your brain, being mad, scatty and even having a yellow minute (See Table 8.2).

Denham and Burton (2003) note that young children are just beginning to realise that affective messages can be sent and that they can explain their emotions. They also add that peers benefit from witnessing and listening to other children's expressions of emotions. Over the course of the program the data evidenced children demonstrating more sophisticated levels of social emotional confidence, especially in relation to giving voice to a wide range

Table 8.2 Feelings vocabulary

PLEASANT	UNPLEASANT
good	lonely
ordinary	sad
happy & super happy	angry
loving	pain
kissing	hurt
hugging	confused
excited	scared
proud	tired
sunshiny	bored
crazy	very very hurt
OK	woozy
silly	crying
funny	nervous
bouncy	lazy
dancing	distracted
peaceful	annoyed
relaxed	shaky
calm	frozen

of emotional feelings, along with strategies that they had to support their capacity to manage their experience in the group. For example:

- coping means finding ways of how your friends can help you be good again.
- I was sad when I came to kindergarten this morning, but when I played with my friend I am happy now.
- I am not even crying today.

As noted by Dacey and Lennon (1998), 'agency is the capacity to act intentionally. When people view their own ability to do something, they assume the freedom to act with intention. Before acting they must believe in their self-efficacy' (p. 181). The findings of this research indicate that the participating children embraced their personal responsibility for naming emotions and willingly engaged in collaborative discussions about social emotional issues.

Enacting relational care and empathy for others and the environment

The concept of empathy can be viewed as the building block for relationships because it refers to an individual's capacity to understand and even embody the perspectives, needs and intentions of others (Gallese, 2003). The research highlighted the capacity of the children to question not just what they knew about care between and for humans, but also their perception of care between humans and the environment. There was extensive evidence through drawing-tellings that the children were able to argue and logically explain their involvement in the care of their friends, the immediate environment and the world. For example:

- When you care you look at someone and listen.
- I am caring for my sister. She is learning to walk and I use my hands to make her feel strong.
- My dad felt like not going to work one day. He works very hard. I made him a vegemite sandwich (for him) and a cup of coffee to help him feel better. After his breakfast he felt better.
- To share you must be kind and listen to a person and ask for something in a nice way.

The teacher guided the children's discussion about caring for others, family, friends and community. She asked the children to express their thoughts about the caring acts that they could enact and the children's responses demonstrate a deep level of care and empathy for those in the community who need support. For example:

- If anything bad happens you can help people.
- You could make a necklace for a hurt friend.
- You can give homeless people some food and pillows and doonas for winter time.
- You can make your friends happy by just listening to them.

The children also expressed wishes for a more sustainable and peaceful future, for example:

- We should melt all the guns and turn them into beautiful things.
- We should connect all the waters of the world.
- Every human is precious.
- Plant 500 trees so that they grow. Never throw rubbish in the Yarra River.
- Read all of the books with your mum so you learn how to look after the world.
- Put special stuff on the world to keep it alive. Ride your bike so it doesn't pollute the air.

Through the drawings of polite/non-polite acts/behaviours the children expressed and created a list of predictable and newly invented polite expressions that were being applied daily in the classroom and revisited on many occasions, mostly in situations that required awareness of cultural practices during meal times, greetings and communication, for example, Excuse me/ May I/Could I/I appreciate this/Oh, this is lovely/My pleasure darling/Just a gentle reminder/Hedgehog's little hands. The drawing-tellings also shed light on how cultural differences impact on individual children's behaviours. For example, during a discussion about politeness individual children shared their personal cultural stories that related to culturally-appropriate practices.

The children were guided to create small cards for their friends and families. On these they identified their feelings towards the recipients, showing courtesy and enacting polite values, for example (Figure 8.1):

- Dear Sienna,

I love you and I like being your cousin. You make me feel happy. Thank you for coming to my birthday party.

- Dear Ada,

You always play with me. Please come to my house and we can play together. I live in Robert Street and my house has a red roof. I grow trees in my garden and also lemon bushes.

The cards were decorated with a range of intricate symbols such as love hearts, flowers, stars, butterflies, suns and bows.

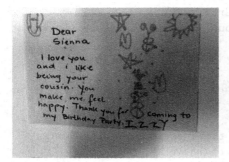

Figure 8.1 Learning to express courtesy and politeness

The teacher's journal shed light on powerful questioning that stimulated the children's articulation of their developing understandings. For example:

- What is polite behaviour?
- How are we polite to others?
- How does it make you feel if someone is unfriendly and impolite to you?

The children were able to identify how their peers from different cultural backgrounds express politeness and what makes their actions different from their own. During the group discussion one child from an Arabic and Asian background commented that 'politeness is being soft with a kind voice when speaking with others, gently bowing and sometimes even closing your eyes'. Private symbols and metaphors as well as real life scenarios were shared amongst the group, for example, the Japanese Tea Ceremony was brought into the curriculum and all of the children had the opportunity to experience the reverence of this traditional ceremony (see Figure 8.2). One child commented, 'quiet, beautiful and friendly spaces and sharing from one pot makes us kind and polite. When you are calm it's easier to be polite because you say your words with kindness'.

Children openly shared their emotions, for example, one child's drawing-telling communicated deeply felt emotion: 'One of my friends look a bit sad, I wonder why?', '[A] lovely veil above me that made me feel calm and relaxed', 'Grace is twirling me in the rain dance and I am feeling happy and excited.' As thinking and emotion work together in life the teaching of social emotional skills draws attention to thinking about intrapersonal and interpersonal interactions, which at times helps the individual child to move beyond their personal emotional experience, knowledge and capacity for regulation. The above comments, as illustrated in Figure 8.3,

Figure 8.2 Showing respect and care through sharing tea

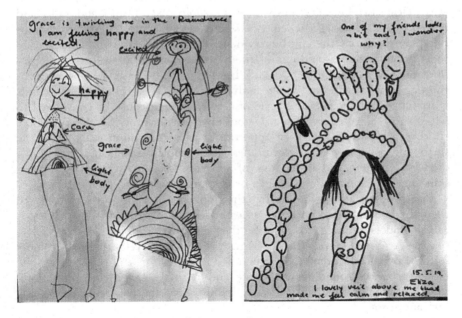

Figure 8.3 Sharing emotions through drawing-telling

draws attention to the young child's capacity to identify the problem, name the physical emotion laden reaction and engage in means to an end and consequential thinking; all important thinking skills which lead to positive social development.

For the young child, the development of empathy for others is ongoing (Feshbach, 1982, Feshbach & Feshbach, 2009) and contingent on developing cognitive and emotional skills that enable the child to not only assume the perspective of another person but also to be able to feel and understand the emotional state of the person or the experience. In this study the children were observed responding empathetically to others and paying attention to their intentions. As noted by Berrol (2006), feeling empathetic is understood to have its roots both in the brain and in the body and in order to share and respond to another person's physical and emotional experience the child needs to first experience it (Feshbach, 1982; Hoffman, 2000).

Appreciating the emotions of self, others and spaces

The data evidenced the children's commitment to appreciating their own emotions and the emotions of their peers. One of the significant outcomes of a collaborative learning experience was the creation of a poster that represented 'listening with your whole body'. The resultant group drawing of a 'good listener' depicted a person listening with his brain ('open brain') eyes ('clear, bright and focused'), ears, whole body ('calm and tall') and heart ('gentle, especially when a person is sad or angry'). Through various role-play situations the children evidenced their capacities to communicate their personal understandings of their own emotions as well as the emotions of their peers. One child said 'listening is more than just hearing it's concentrating with your whole body; you need to listen to your friends with your whole body'. This style of active learning could be considered to fall within the category of social emotional problem-solving theory, where children are provided with an opportunity to encode information from the surroundings, interpret it, form ideas and problem-solve solutions. Children become engaged in a range of activities to support growing understandings of their own and other's behaviours within the social setting.

The children also demonstrated their appreciation for and sensitivity to their surroundings and in doing so extended the reach of their social emotional understandings to include the appreciation for the emotion of spaces. A 'Voice Level Chart' (Figure 8.4) was developed with colours selected by the children to correspond to noise levels; white being the softest, whispering sound, blue – soft and normal, green – optimal loud sound, orange – very loud but not alarming and the red being the shouting, angry sound.

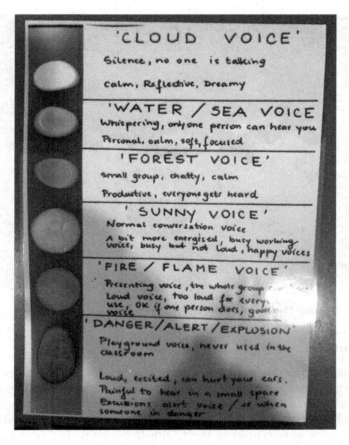

Figure 8.4 Voice Level Chart created by children

The significance of silence was also identified as being important and children evidenced their interest in practicing meditation and creating soft, quiet, peaceful spaces. The data uncovered how unique sensory materials such as stones, crystals and glass discs that were provided for open-ended play stimulated the children to metaphorically express their social and emotional connections. Children also created a Mandala of Silences (Figure 8.5) using their own bodies, which communicated individual and collaborative ideas about spiritual and emotional connections to place and people.

Figure 8.5 Outdoor Mandala of Silence created by children

Conclusion

This chapter has presented evidence that highlights the capacity of young children to deeply reflect upon and make comment about emotions and relationships. What has been uncovered is that the children embraced the concepts of Care, Open-communication, Politeness and Empathy that were central to the COPE-R program. For young children to come to know their own emotions and those of family, friends and teachers requires intentional teaching and experiences that are thoughtfully developed to enable positive social emotional functioning. Through the implementation of the COPE-R program which included teacher scaffolding and purposeful integration of children's personal interests and experiences the children had the opportunity to engage in social emotional problem-solving that led to a range of affective interchanges and sustained positive engagement with peers. The focus was placed on the how and why of thoughtful, caring and empathetic actions which were identified as being important to ensure harmonious living. Through multimodal explorations the children gave voice to their emotional understandings, they enacted relational care and empathy for others and the environment, and they demonstrated their appreciation for emotions of self, others and spaces. Phrases evidenced in the data such as, Play together/I love being polite and sharing/Join in play/

Humans care/The forests live and care for us/Love your friends/We love the Earth/We are tender/We are strong, demonstrate the children's capacity to embrace their emotional life and relationships with others that are imbued with contextually relevant values, beliefs and practices (Calloway-Thomas, 2010; Dachyshyn, 2015) such as empathy, reciprocity, generosity, kindness and joy.

Take home messages

- Pre-school teachers can play an important role to foster prosocial emotional development in young children.
- Provide children with regular contact with nurturing, caring, respectful and attentive adults who construct many and varied opportunities for children to identify their feelings and the feelings of others.
- Help children to give voice to their emotions and help them to consider the feelings of others and, importantly, consequences of their actions.
- Through explicit use of vocabulary that describes emotions, teachers can encourage children to identify, problem-solve and think of positive alternative ways for managing and resolving challenging social emotional situations that are stressful and cause conflict.

References

Allison, C., Baron-Cohen, S., Wheelwright, S. J., Stone, M. H., & Muncer, S. J. (2011). Psychometric analysis of the Empathy Quotient (EQ). *Personality and Individual Differences, 51*(7), 829–835.

Bandura, A. (1969). Social-learning theory of identificatory processes. In D. A. Goslin (Ed.), *Handbook of socialisation theory and research* (pp. 213–262). Chicago: Rand McNally.

Baron-Cohen, S., & Wheelwright, S. (2004). The Empathy Quotient: An investigation of adults with Asperger syndrome or high functioning autism, and normal sex differences. *Journal of Autism and Developmental Disorders, 34*(2), 163–175.

Bassett, H., Denham, S., & Zinsser, K. (2012). Early childhood teachers as socializers of young children's emotional competence. *Early Childhood Education, 40*, 137–143.

Belacchi, C., & Farina, E. (2012). Feeling and thinking of others: Affective and cognitive empathy and emotion comprehension in prosocial/hostile pre-schoolers. *Aggressive Behavior, 38*(2), 150–165. doi:10.1002/ab.21415

Berrol, C. (2006). Neuroscience meets dance/movement therapy: Mirror neurons, the therapeutic process and empathy. *The Arts in Psychotherapy, 3*, 302–315.

Brackett, M. A., Rivers, S. E., Reyes, M. R., & Salovey, P. (2012). Enhancing academic performance and social and emotional competence with the RULER feeling words curriculum. *Learning and Individual Differences, 22*(2), 218–224. doi:10.1016/j.lindif.2010.10.002

Burdelski, M. (2010). Socializing politeness routines: Action, other-orientation, and embodiment in a Japanese pre-school. *Journal of Pragmatics*, *42*, 1606–1621. doi:10.1016/j.pragma.2009.11.007

Calloway-Thomas, C. (2010). *Empathy in the global world: An intercultural perspective.* Thousand Oaks, CA: Sage.

Carreras, M. R., Braza, P., Muñoz, J. M., Braza, F., Azurmendi, A., Pascual-Sagastizabal, E., ... Sánchez-Martín, J. R. (2014). Aggression and prosocial behaviors in social conflicts mediating the influence of cold social intelligence and affective empathy on children's social preference. *Scandinavian Journal of Psychology*, *55*(4), 371–379. doi:10.1111/sjop.12126

Caselman, T. (2007). *Teaching children empathy, the social emotion: Lessons, activities and reproducible worksheets (K-6) that teach how to "Step Into Other's Shoes".* South Carolina: YouthLight Incorporated.

Chen, G., & Fu, X. (2003). Effects of multimodal information on learning performance and judgment of learning. *Journal of Educational Computing Research*, *29*(3), 349–362.

Dacey, J. S., & Lennon, K. H. (1998). *Understanding creativity. The interplay of biological, psychological, and social factors.* California: Jossey-Bass.

Dachyshyn, D. M. (2015). Being mindful, heartful, and ecological in early years care and education. *Contemporary Issues in Early Childhood*, *16*(1), 32–41. doi:10.1177/1463949114566756

Decety, J. (2011). The neuroevolution of empathy. *Annals of the New York Academy of Sciences*, *1231*, 35–45.

DEECD - Department of Education and Early Childhood Development. (2009). *Victorian early years learning and development framework.* Melbourne: Early Childhood Strategy Division, Department of Early Childhood Development and Victorian Curriculum Authority.

DEEWR - Department of Education, Employment and Workplace. (2009). *Belonging, Being & Becoming. The Early Years Learning Framework for Australia.* ACT: Commonwealth Copyright Division.

DEEWR, EYLF. (2009). *Belonging, Being & Becoming: The Early Years Learning Framework for Australia* (pp. c2009). Canberra: Dept. of Education, Employment and Workplace Relations for the Council of Australian Governments.

DeMeulenaere, M. (2015). Promoting social and emotional learning in pre-school. *Dimensions of Early Childhood*, *43*(1), 8–10.

Denham, S. A. (1998). *Emotional development in young children.* New York: Guilford.

Denham, S. A., & Burton, R. (2003). *Social and emotional prevention and intervention programming for pre-schoolers.* New York: Kluwer Academic/Plenum Publishers.

Durlak, J. A., Weissberg, R. P., Dymnicki, A. B., Taylor, R. D., & Schellinger, K. B. (2011). The impact of enhancing students' social and emotional learning: A meta-analysis of school-based universal interventions. *Child Development*, *82*(1), 405–432. doi:10.1111/j.1467-8624.2010.01564.x

Eisenberg, N., Cumberland, A., & Spinrad, T. L. (1998). Parental socialization of emotion. *Psychological Inquiry*, *9*, 241–273.

Fadel, C. (2008). *Multimodal learning through media: What the research says.* San Jose, CA: Cisco Systems.

Feshbach, N. D. (1982). Sex differences in empathy and social behavior in children. In N. Eisenberg (Ed.), *The development of prosocial behavior* (pp. 315–338). New York: Academic Press.

Feshbach, N. D., & Feshbach, S. (2009). Empathy and education. In J. Decety & W. Ickes (Eds.), *The social neuroscience of empathy* (pp. 85–98). Cambridge, MA: The MIT Press.

Flook, L., Goldberg, S. B., Pinger, L., & Davidson, R. J. (2015). Promoting prosocial behavior and self-regulatory skills in pre-school children through a mindfulness-based kindness curriculum. *Developmental Psychology*, 54(1): 44.

Frydenberg, E., & Deans, J. (2011). *The Early Years Coping Cards*. Melbourne and Australia: Australia Council for Educational Research.

Gallese, V. (2003). The roots of empathy: The shared manifold hypothesis and the neural basis of intersubjectivity [Electronic version]. *Psychopathology*, 36(36), 171–180.

Havighurst, S. S., Wilson, K. R., Harle, A. E., Prior., M. R., & Kehoe., C. (2010). Tuning in to kids: Improving emotion socialization practices in parents of preschool children – findings from a community trial. *Journal of Child Psychology & Psychiatry*, 51(12), 1342–1350. doi:10.1111/j.1469-7610.2010.02303.x

Hoffman, M. L. (2000). *Empathy and moral development: Implications for caring and justice*. Cambridge: Cambridge University Press.

Jans, M. (2004). Children as citizens: Towards a contemporary notion of child participation. *Childhood. A Global Journal of Child Research*, 11(1), 27–44.

Mayer, R. E. (2003). Elements of a science of e-learning. *Journal of Educational Computing Research*, 29(3), 297–313.

Merriman, B., & Guerin, S. (2006). Using children's drawings as data in child-centred research. *Irish Journal of Psychology*, 27(1–2), 48–57.

Miyamoto, K., Huerta, M. C., & Kubacka, K. (2015). Fostering social and emotional skills for well-being and social progress. *European Journal of Education*, 50 (2), 147–159.

Moreno, R., & Mayer, R. (2007). Interactive multimodal learning environments. *Educational Psychological Review*, 19(3), 309–326.

Mortari, L. (2011). Thinking silently in the woods: Listening to children speaking about emotion. *European Early Childhood Education Research Journal*, 19(3), 345–356. doi:10.1080/1350293X.2011.597966

Moustakas, C. E. (1994). *Phenomenological research methods*. London: Sage.

New Zealand, Ministry of Education. (1996). *Te Whāriki early childhood curriculum*. Wellington, New Zealand: Learning Media Limited.

Nutbrown, C. (2011). *Threads of thinking: schemas and young children's learning*. London: SAGE.

Page, J. (2007) Children's discourses of emotions: Rethinking citizenship. Unpublished doctoral dissertation, The University of Melbourne, Victoria.

Parker, A. E., Mathis, E. T., & Kupersmidt, J. B. (2013). How is this child feeling? Pre-school-aged children's ability to recognize emotion in faces and body poses. *Early Education & Development*, 24(2), 188–211. doi:10.1080/10409289.2012.657536

Paulus, M., Licata, M., Kristen, S., Thoermer, C., Woodward, A., & Sodian, B. (2015). Social understanding and self-regulation predict pre-schoolers' sharing with friends and disliked peers: A longitudinal study. *International Journal of Behavioral Development*, 39(1), 53–64.

Perkins, K. (2014). Parents and teachers: Working together to foster children's learning. *The Research Digest, QCT, 2014*(10). Retrieved from http://www.qct.edu.au

Piscetelli, B., & McArdle, F. (1999). Children have rights: Lessons for teachers and the wider world [Electronic version]. *International Journal of Early Childhood, 31* (1), 60–67.

Rafaila, E. (2015). The competent teacher for teaching emotional intellgence. *Procedia - Social and Behavioral Sciences, 180*, 953–957. doi:10.1016/j. sbspro.2015.02.253

Roberts, H. (2000). Listening to children: And hearing them. In P. Christensen & A. James (Eds.), *Research with children: Perspectives and practices* (pp. 225–240). London: Falmer Press.

Rogoff, B. (1994). Developing understanding of the idea of communities of learners. *Mind, Culture and Activity, 1*(4), 209–229.

Rogoff, B. (1998). Cognition as a collaborative process. In W. Damon (Ed.), *Handbook of child psychology: Vol. 2. Cognition, perception, and language* (pp. 679–744). Hoboken, NJ: John Wiley & Sons Inc.

Rosenthal, M., & Gatt, L. (2010). 'Learning to Live Together': Training early childhood educators to promote socio-emotional competence of toddlers and pre-school children. *European Early Childhood Education Research Journal, 18*(3), 373–390.

Schwenck, C., Göhle, B., Hauf, J., Warnke, A., Freitag, C. M., & Schneider, W. (2014). Cognitive and emotional empathy in typically developing children: The influence of age, gender, and intelligence. *European Journal of Developmental Psychology, 11*(1), 63–76. doi:10.1080/17405629.2013.808994

Shah, P., & Freedman, E. G. (2003). Visuospatial cognition in electronic learning. *Journal of Educational Computing Research, 29*(3), 315–324.

van Manen, M. (1990). *Researching lived experience*. London: University of West Ontario.

Wright, S. (2007a). Graphic-narrative play: Young children's authoring through drawing and telling. *International Journal of Education and the Arts, 8*, 1–28.

Wright, S. (2007b). Young Children's meaning-making through drawing and 'telling': Analogies to filmic textual features. *Australian Journal of Early Childhood, 321* (4), 37–48.

Wu, M. Y., Alexander, M. A., Frydenberg, E., & Deans, J. (2019). *Teacher experience matters: Social Emotional Learning in the early years*. Australian Educational Researchers.

Chapter 9

Embedding SEL within the curriculum

Partnerships with communities

Sophia Stirling

'I feel good when I go to MP {elder person's residence}. At first, I didn't feel so good. I feel shy, but I just got over it. I knew them 'cause we kept going.'

— *Ellie, 5-year-old*

'I helped Mary get bingos when we play bingo. I got the coloured lids for her. It is fun at MP 'cause we see the neighbours and I get to talk to them and I listen to them.'

—*Janet, 4-year-old*

Overview

This chapter illustrates how young children can develop social and emotional learning through involvement in a community partnership program that fosters relationships across generations. An intergenerational program between a class of children aged 3 to 5 years old attending an early learning centre and elderly residents from a nearby residential home (the Program) will be used throughout this chapter as an example of its positive impact on learning. A brief discussion of the theoretical underpinnings of intergenerational programs is provided that links directly with the techniques used in our Program. The intent is to provide readers with insights and inspiration for their own implementations.

The key tenets of our curriculum and pedagogical practice are outlined as they relate to social and emotional learning and development. Additionally, two case studies and behavioural tasks with research-proven benefits from international intergenerational programs are presented. These can be used as a framework or examples for developing an intergenerational curriculum.

Assessment of children's learning and progress, along with feedback from families, is included in this chapter as an illustration of ways to evaluate the impact of an intergenerational program in achieving its aim of promoting respectful caring relationships and well-being in early childhood.

Challenging age segregation

Since the Industrial Revolution, many societies have seen a significant shift in relationships as a result of increased life expectancy and more people spending time in age-segregated institutions. With modern people living in an increasingly age-segregated society, there is less opportunity for meaningful interactions across age stratifications.

Minichiello and Jamieson (2006) predict 'ageism will become one of the major social challenges of the 21st century', as older people continue to be devalued and discriminated against because of their age attribute. Negative stereotypes and misconceptions in children about older adults can result in stigma, discrimination and exclusion of those in communities and meaningful activities (Galbraith, Larkin, Moorhouse & Oomen, 2015).

Intergenerational programs have been growing in practice and interest around the world and programs have been piloted in the United States, Europe and the United Kingdom as a means of combating the growing social challenge of ageism. They have shown to have a positive impact on children's perceptions of older adults and the aging process (Cartmel et al., 2018; Low, Russell, McDonald & Kauffman, 2015; Gigliotti, Morris, Smock, Jarrott & Graham, 2005). Furthermore, children who engage in intergenerational programs are more positive about older people when they have frequent and regular contact with them. This is a recurring theme throughout the literature.

Social and emotional benefits from intergenerational programs

Research conducted by Femia, Zarit, Blair, Jarrott and Bruno (2008) looked at evaluating the potential impact of intergenerational programming on children's social emotional development, behaviour, school performance and attitude toward older adults. Through face-to-face interviews and surveys from teachers, they compared children's social and emotional development between children engaged in an intergenerational program and children engaged in a single-generational program. Results showed that the children who participated in intergenerational programs had 'higher levels of social acceptance, a greater willingness to help and greater empathy for older adults, slightly more positive attitudes, and better able to self-regulate their behaviour than children from the single-generation program' (Femia et al., 2008). Additionally, research by Heyman, Gutheil and White-Ryan (2011) also measured pre-school children's attitudes towards older adults and found that children from intergenerational programs had overall more positive attitudes to older adults compared to children from single-generational programs.

Theory of intergenerational programs

Intergenerational programs show that well thought out programs reduce prejudice between pre-schoolers and elders (Femia et al., 2008; Low et al., 2015). Conversely, poorly designed programs can have a negative impact on both parties.

To ensure the intergenerational program has a long-lasting positive impact, programs must be thoughtfully implemented, and pedagogy is key to this. Particularly important is designing a curriculum that emphasises the establishment of respectful relationships (DEEWR, 2009).

The following is an overview of some of the major theories which provide the basis for intergenerational learning and inform pedagogical and curriculum design.

Contact theory

The most commonly used and discussed theory relevant to intergenerational programs is contact theory (Kuehne & Melville, 2014). Pettigrew and Tropp (2006) state that the application of contact theory typically leads to a reduction in prejudice between different social groups. Contact theory asserts that under certain conditions intergenerational programs facilitate positive attitudinal change in perceptions between the generations. When appropriate conditions are implemented, interpersonal contact can be an effective method for reducing prejudice or discrimination between age groups.

Contact theory asserts that prejudice will reduce when specific features of the contact situation are present (Kuehne & Melville, 2014). These include;

- Equal group status; this occurs when adults and children are given active roles in the program.
- Common goals; this is when there is a mutual goal of building relationships engaging in participants' current abilities and interests.
- Cooperation; this pertains to the physical setting and layout is critical for cooperation between intergenerational partners; materials should be arranged for intergenerational pairs and close physical proximity to promote collaboration and teamwork to achieve a mutual goal (for instance in playing a game or engaging in a portrait lesson).
- Support from authorities, law or custom; in practice, this means staff from each program meet to plan, feedback, implement and evaluate the program. Additionally, families are important stakeholders and receive regular (daily) communication about the program. It is important to consider the designation of staff responsibility for intergenerational activities

to support programs and promote the sustainability of the program (as most IG programs last less than 2 years) (Hamilton et al., 1999).

Pettigrew (2016) adds to contact theory, stating that intergroup contact is more effective and prejudice is ameliorated when it facilitates mechanisms for friendship such as self-disclosure, which is best achieved through repeated contact. Pettigrew called this 'opportunity for friendships'.

ELC intergenerational program

The setting where the intergenerational program described in this chapter has been implemented is at an ELC attached to a University in Metropolitan Melbourne, Australia. It is a research and demonstration kindergarten. The centre serves the children of the University's faculty, staff and students. There are 180 3- to 5-year-old children enrolled full-time or part-time over the year and 89 children taught across five classrooms per day. The centre engages in project-based learning through a number of multimodal and multidisciplinary inquiry projects and follows the national Early Years Learning Framework (DEEWR, 2009) and the Victorian Early Years Learning and Development Framework (DEECD, 2009). Each class engages in environmental and community projects throughout the year.

Our program logistics

Our intergenerational program takes place between the ELC and a nearby residential aged care facility, MP. The ELC and MP are across the road from one another and the aged care residents who are referred to collectively as 'the neighbours' in our Program.

The Program began as a pilot in 2016, where one class of 20 children (aged 3 to 5 years) attended MP for an hour each week. Over the course of the year, 20 residents volunteered to participate in the Program. Since the 2016 pilot, the Program has expanded to two classes of 20 children each participating in alternating visits fortnightly with ten consistent resident volunteers supplemented by another ten residents participating semi-regularly. Residents range from 65 to 100 years old and have varying health needs, levels of mobility and cognitive ability.

Two lead teachers and a support teacher from the ELC participate in the Program and liaise with two lifestyle coordinators from MP. The Program commences from orientation (mid-February) until December. Children with reported sickness must be absent from the Program for the duration of their sickness. The Program does not continue during school holidays when lead teachers are away. If a lead teacher or a support teacher are absent, residents are invited to visit at the ELC to ensure teacher-to-student ratios are maintained and there is minimal interruption to the Program.

Children enrolled in the Program are selected randomly and parents are informed about the intergenerational program during a parent information evening at the beginning of the year. While no parents have opted out of the Program, some families have specifically requested their child to be a part of the Program due to their child's lack of contact with older generations.

Parents are provided with program updates through a daily diary as well as through informal conversations with staff. Parents have opportunities to meet the residents at social events throughout the year, such as the mid-year choir performance.

Program aims

The purpose of the intergenerational program with MP is to build and develop relationships and reduce the separation between generations. The Program aims to enrich relationships, exchange knowledge and increase skills to benefit well-being across the generations, which has been shown to increase social connections within communities; develop interest in culture and history; and create 'broad social empathy across groups ... that challenged stereotypical views of "the other"' (Gallagher & Fitzpatrick, 2018).

Program evaluation

The effectiveness of the Program in achieving these aims was evaluated primarily through feedback from stakeholders, direct observations of interactions and relationships over the course of the Program, and reflective drawing-tellings from the children.

Feedback was sought throughout the year from aged care staff regarding the interactions between children and the aged care residents. At several points during the Program, teachers conducted group feedback sessions with the aged care residents on their experience of the Program and suggestions for improvements and activities to undertake with the children. Parents were afforded the opportunity to comment regularly on the Program via an online daily diary documenting the visits. Additionally, a formal end-of-year survey was conducted to assess parents' views of the Program and the effects they had observed on their child.

The second key component of evaluation comprised of observations of children's interactions and how they progressed over the course of the Program in terms of their level of participation in the Program, willingness to engage in conversation and depth of conversation with the residents.

To evaluate the children's experience of the Program, at the end of each visit the children participated in a reflective drawing-telling. They were asked to draw something they remembered from their visit that day. After their drawing the children dictated their words about their picture while the teacher recorded verbatim the words each child used to talk about their picture. These drawing-tellings provided an insight into the thoughts and views of each child's experiences of what they valued or remembered from the experience. Deans and Wright (2018) talk about how reflective drawing-tellings allow for reflective thinking to recall, review and relate an experience immediately after having had the experience. It is a way of synthesising information, validating learning, developing memory, contextualising learning, as well as promoting the children's ability to articulate their learning.

Reciprocal visits and tours

There is evidence that intergroup contact is more positive when it facilitates mechanisms for friendship such as self-disclosure. This is best achieved through repeated contact in a friendly atmosphere, such as through games and reciprocal visits (Cartmel et al., 2018).

During the Program some of the neighbours would take the class on a tour around MP, showing the children the different dining, lounge and bedroom spaces, which opened up conversations about interests. Through this self-disclosure the children developed a more intimate knowledge of their neighbours as people, including their interests and personal day-to-day experiences. Additionally, touring through the residential quarters meant that the children were able to locate the neighbours geographically within the community. For example, one neighbour pointed out her window which overlooked the children's classrooms, and several children began adding MP as a locale on maps they drew of the local area.

Engaging in reciprocal visits allowed the program leader to ease the children into the intergenerational project. This focused the project on relationships – not just the new space. Thus, throughout the year, we invited the neighbours to come and spend time at the ELC. Children would show their classroom and outdoor environments to the residents and engage them in their learning and play spaces. This empowered the children to take on a role to teach the residents about what they had been learning as well as share their portfolios. It cast the children as a 'host' as they took on social etiquette roles, such as taking the neighbours on a tour of their environment.

Intergenerational program content

The design of our curriculum is one which considers how to maximise relationships as quickly as possible so as to foster respect and collaboration, which in turn develops mutual trust and connection. Activities varied in frequency and duration from regular (music, singing, gardening and storytelling) to one-off activities (shared concerts and performances). Each visit provided an opportunity for the children to engage in social and emotional learning, with explicit teaching around manners, politeness and social etiquette. The following is an overview of the curriculum and some vignettes (see Figures 9.1 to 9.9) of what happened from these experiences.

Social etiquette

Throughout the Program, we incorporated intentional teaching around social etiquette. Before, during and after visiting our neighbours we engaged in whole group discussions and role-play around how to greet neighbours, remembering our manners, asking neighbours how their weekend was, shaking their hands and saying 'thank you for having me' at the end of each visit.

We had discussions around the need to project our voice more as one of our neighbours was deaf in one ear, while also remembering that when we go through the residential care environment, we needed to remember to take our hats off. Some of our neighbours sleep in their chairs during our visits, which is an opportunity to discuss and practise how to be respectful

Figure 9.1 Children shaking hands with their neighbours to thank them for the visit

around our neighbours while they slept. One of our neighbours was wheel-chair bound due to a chronically injured leg which always needed to be outstretched. This meant that the children needed to be aware of making sure that they did not go too close to his leg as touch could have hurt it. Additionally, when some of our residents needed to leave the room and the room was crowded with tables, chairs and people, we alerted the children to make sure they could help move things out of the way to aid the neighbour's safe pathway. Social etiquette skills were always presenting themselves, depending on the physical requirements of the neighbours and the layout of the room.

After engaging in the Program for the duration of a term (12 weeks), the children were asked what they do at MP; one child's response included;

> (When we go to MP) I help pack up. Like stuff they don't want around when they're walking, because they don't want to slip. I help pack up.
>
> *Aurora, 4-year-old*

Another child commented;

> I like doing nice things like saying "Hello, how are you?"
>
> *Tom, 4-year-old*

Narrative and storytelling

Storytelling was an opportunity for the children and residents to learn about each other's lives. This can take different forms such as formal interviews, show and tell, shared reading and spontaneous informal conversations between the children and the residents. In particular, it is important to leave time for informal communication to occur in a safe and calm environment (Cartmel et al., 2018).

On a few occasions we engaged in shared morning tea and it was during these less structured engagements that there was opportunity for spontaneous conversation and self-disclosure. During one of the shared morning tea gatherings, one of the residents started telling the children about how at 4 years old he used to ride a horse to school with his siblings. Opportunity from these conversations sparked curriculum ideas for the Program; specifically, from this conversation we set out to interview and learn about our neighbours' childhoods. As a class, we interviewed our neighbours over the term, collecting the childhood memories of the residents and collating these into a book. Questions revolved around where they grew up, their favourite foods, how they got to school and any other stories they wanted to share about their childhood. This also was an effective means of teaching the children about social roles and the similarities and differences in peoples' experiences through history. The interview process also gave the children opportunities to practise asking questions about things that were important to them as well as how to connect with people to obtain new knowledge. Collating the stories into a book also gave the parents insight into the Program and what the children were getting out of it. In essence, having opportunities to listen and learn about our neighbours' childhoods was a key part of challenging children's perceptions of the elderly, as it teaches them that the MP residents were once children, which helps establish empathy and allows opportunities for friendship.

Show and tell was also an opportunity for the residents to learn from the children. As the children became more confident in the neighbours' space, they asked to stand at the front to address everyone in the room to share news or show an object. This offered a back and forth dialogue between the residents and the children, as residents would ask questions

Figure 9.2 The final product; a collection of childhood memories made into a book

from the children to gain more information about their stories. At times a child would be asked to share some news, but instead would get up and tell a joke, which developed into an impromptu back and forth joke-telling session between the children and adults. Sharing humour is both an icebreaker and builds comradery between people and highlights the comfort and confidence that children experience in and with their neighbours.

Shared reading exercises also served to show the children that they can access learning from elderly residents. The children chose their favourite book to share with a resident, who would read to them and the children would bring their ELC portfolios or diaries with them to share their work with the residents. This reciprocity in sharing and learning showed both generations that they could learn from each other and promotes inclusion.

Historical/cultural – reminiscing project

Teaching the children that older people have valuable knowledge to pass on was an important part of the Program. We aimed to show the children that all people offer new insights and knowledge of the world and that learning can take place at any stage of life and be 'facilitated by people

Figure 9.3 Children engaging in shared reading with their neighbours

who are not trained, paid or acknowledged as teachers' (Boström, 2003; Gallagher & Fitzpatrick, 2018). We engaged in a reminiscing project, using specifically chosen artefacts as catalysts for conversations to highlight the changes in technology and social relationships through time. Historical and cultural objects included glass milk bottles, cameras, radios, kitchenware, toys such as spinning tops, typewriters, photographs of cars and radio vignettes of superman comics. Over the course of a term we would take these objects over to MP in a basket and present each item one at a time for a group discussion. Firstly, we asked the children their thoughts about each object before the residents would go on to explain what the object was or share personal stories about them.

This is D in his wheelchair. This is the tray with cups and a tea pot. This is the tea lady bringing drinks. This is the basket with things in it. We looked at things in the basket because things a long time ago, they had them.

Yolanda, 4-year-old

During a conversation around glass milk bottles, it turned out that one of the residents had been a milkman with a horse and cart. He described to the children the process of delivering the milk and collecting the empty glass bottles. This was a catalyst for discussions comparing food delivery systems today, as well as looking at food packaging and recycling versus reusing. Conversely, when looking at different technologies such as telephones and televisions, the children explained to some of the residents about YouTube, iPads and Google.

Sometimes calendar events would be a catalyst for conversation, highlighting the changes in society over decades. During a visit which

Figure 9.4 A drawing-telling from a child, depicting the MP environment after engaging in a reminiscing lesson, looking at historical objects

coincided with International Women's Day, one of our residents told the children about her experience as a female studying medicine in a male-dominated industry during the 1960s. She told the children how her lecturer had told her that she was taking the place of a man. Some of the children were outraged at her treatment and this came through in feedback from the parents' comments about the intergenerational program;

> *Annabel still talks about International Women's Day. Every now and then she randomly says to me "Did you know that in the olden days women couldn't vote?" or something like that.*
>
> ELC Parent, 2018

The sharing of knowledge between the generations through storytelling and discussions around historical and modern artefacts highlights the current literature on children and adult pedagogy that encourages best practices in the Program. 'The pedagogical concept is based on the premise that both generations can learn from each other, the role of the teacher and student being undertaken within both groups' (Cartmel et al., 2018).

Fine arts and literacy

Eisner (2002) highlights that the arts are a bridge for connecting communities. Through shared painting, drawing, craft activities and music the children and neighbours shared many experiences.

Fine art activities meant that there was close physical proximity between the children and older adults. We purposefully organised activities for the children and residents to observe one another closely through portrait drawing. This encouraged residents and children to look at each other's features.

Engaging in clay modelling also meant that we would create collaborative pieces which could be shared in the different environments.

For birthday celebrations the children drew collaborative portraits of the residents, or paintings of something they knew their neighbours enjoyed. For instance, it was no secret that a particular resident loved Elvis and the children created a portrait of Elvis with a guitar as a gift for him. Similarly, another resident's favourite song was 'True Colors' by Cyndi Lauper. For her birthday the children wrote out the lyrics to the song and drew corresponding illustrations to create a 'True Colors' book. Upon receiving this gift on her birthday, she broke out into song to the children. This highlights the reciprocity with the arts in connecting the two communities.

Literacy experiences also took the form of card writing, especially as the year drew to a close. The children wrote messages to the neighbours and delivered these in person to say thank you for the year.

Figure 9.5 The children created a book with illustrations and lyrics of a resident's favourite song. This was an opportunity for the children to learn and respond to another's interests

Music

Music is an active social phenomenon that 'can be used to help create flourishing communities in which the diversity of individual difference is celebrated, and support is shared' (Steele, 2016). Music enhances connectedness and Gosine, Hawksley and LeMessurier Quinn (2017) talk about the importance of music-making in building community engagement. We used music to learn about the residents' favourite songs, reminisce, practise performing new musical skills, as well as to participate in community performance events.

To make music accessible between the children and the residents, at the beginning of the year, the children are set the task to research each resident's favourite songs. This informed part of our curriculum throughout the year as the children engaged in listening and learning these songs to share with our neighbours. On one occasion, the children sang 'True Colors', a favourite song of one of the residents, and she reported back in a letter that that was one of her favourite experiences during the intergenerational program. For birthday celebrations the children gathered around the residents and sang the birthday song, complete with age-corresponding claps (some of these claps included counting to 93 which had residents in hysterics). Other ritualistic singing included the neighbours singing theme songs from competing local football teams to teach the children 'their' team's song.

For some of the children who were learning an instrument, our time at MP was an opportunity for them to share a new-found skill and perform these in front of an appreciative group. Again, this was an opportunity for the children to develop their confidence in being in front of an audience.

Music and dance performances were a meaningful experience for both the performers (the children) and the audience (the residents). For some of the residents, these events were their only opportunities to be invited and involved in public musical events. Several times a year the ELC performed choir and choreographed dance concerts to families. On these occasions we also invited the neighbours to be among the audience. These events offered the children the experience of performing in front of an audience and afterwards it meant that families were about to meet and put a face to the residents. During one rehearsal, a resident wiped away tears as he watched the children performing their dance, highlighting the emotional impact of including the residents in these events. Additionally, after a performance a parent came to a teacher to confirm the name of a resident, as she connected that he was an old family friend of her mother. This highlights the opportunities for connection and belonging through shared-art events.

> *That's in dance class. Our neighbours, they are watching us and they are singing with us.*
>
> *Kalam, 4-year-old*

Games

Engaging in games was both a means for creating a friendly atmosphere and also fostering cooperation between the children and the residents. We engaged in regular sessions of bingo (and sometimes physical games such as throwing balloons or games of quoits) over the course of the project. Bingo was an opportunity for the residents to teach the children the game, but as the children could see and move better they helped the residents play the game, highlighting a reciprocal benefit for both groups. In one instance, a child was supporting his partner in bingo as she couldn't see the images. He was able to tell her what images were being displayed and inform her if they had the image on their card. Thus, bingo facilitated shared communication and cooperation between partners. Additionally, during bingo, the images of different cards were a catalyst for conversation and we consciously paused to allow natural conversation to take place between the generations. These sorts of informal spaces allowed opportunities for dialogue and informal encounters.

Gardening

The garden is an example of a physical setting which promotes collaboration and teamwork to achieve a mutual goal. Gardening is a strong passion for some of our neighbours but some of the MP garden is raised in high garden beds, making it difficult to access. We set out to turn these gardens into more enjoyable spaces. The children carried out the physical work under the neighbours' instruction. During springtime, flower arranging was popular with residents and children and was used as an activity to educate about gifts and giving. Children brought flowers from their garden and arranged them with neighbours to make spring posies to give as gifts to the neighbours. Some children needed support to understand that when giving the posies they were permanent gifts, as some children wanted to take them home for themselves.

Figure 9.6 A drawing-telling from a child, depicting the residents during a shared music class

Figure 9.7 Children engaging in collaborative bingo with the neighbours

Death, compassion and partnership

Death can be considered a social taboo and the complex range of perspectives regarding death, dying and bereavement make it difficult for teachers to know how to engage with it in the curriculum. Kennedy, Keeffe, Gardner and Farrelly (2017) talk about the need to discuss death in school communities and give expression to grieving so as to enhance compassion, connectedness and support. The nature of significant interaction with the elderly can bring up the opportunity to integrate the topic of death in the curriculum.

A 93-year-old resident had joined the intergenerational program for a term and over the school holidays he passed away. When MP staff informed teachers about his passing, we were wondering how to approach the topic with the children. We decided to inform the children at a group time, relaying the information; that he had fallen out of his bed and then his body became sick and stopped working. We also made the point that it 'was his time' to ensure specifically what happened was relevant to only him at that time.

Kennedy et al. (2017) highlights that storytelling is an effective strategy to aid bereavement and end of life. Storytelling or sharing experiences of

Figure 9.8 Children helping in the garden

dying, death or loss enable people to 'swap stories and experiences with other people (as it reduces) a sense of isolation' (Kellehear, 2014).

To give expression to the children's understanding of what happened and what they took away from the visit that day, the children engaged in a drawing-telling. One child drew Leslie falling out of bed and dying, while other children drew Lindsay in the cemetery. Other children didn't represent Lindsay at all in their drawings. Additionally, we wrote cards to Lindsay's friends to say sorry to hear about his passing.

End-of-year survey feedback from the overall intergenerational program showed that families frequently acknowledged the topic of death being engaged in the curriculum and the flow on this had in discussions at home with families. Many families stated that 'aging and death' were key learnings from the Program. One family commented that their child learnt;

> *Knowledge about aging, life and death; one person of the MP died and it was an opportunity for the children to talk about it with us, and the teachers (without the huge emotional burden that is often associated with a loss of close relatives).*

> *ELC Parent, 2017*

Figure 9.9 A drawing-telling from a child, following a class discussion about the passing of one of our neighbours

> *This is L. He's falling and then he died and then he turned into a star. And then he was a star forever.*
>
> *Nelson, 4-year-old*

Case study: the struggling child

Initially it can be overwhelming for some children to go and meet the residents in an unfamiliar environment. To transition the children into the project we prepared the children through storytelling (we read 'Wilfrid Gordon McDonald Partridge' by Mem Fox), engaged in social role-play and walks in the community past MP, pointing out its proximity from the ELC. Despite efforts made to ease the transition, on one of our first visits a child had a screaming 'melt-down' just as we entered MP. Looking at the residents she screamed 'They're old! They have old eyes!' and was clinging on to a teacher. Some of the residents tried to put her at ease by coming up and trying to talk to her but this escalated her emotions and a teacher took her to a secluded garden to settle. While there, one of the residential staff went to see if she could help. She sat with her and had a chat about the neighbours and after the visit the child was much more at ease about visiting and getting to know the neighbours became her focus for the next visit which eased her transition into the residential space. Over the coming weeks, the child's confidence increased so much in the space she even asked to perform a song in front of everyone. Her parents commented about the progress she had made over time in her visits at MP.

My child has had little exposure to elderly people, other than her grandparents, and at first she was quite apprehensive about the visits. Now she is comfortable with the visits to MP and also in the company of a group of elderly people which has coincidentally happened a couple of times since the ELC project started.

ELC Parent, 2018

Interestingly, when asked to articulate how she felt about going to MP, the child was also able to state the progress of her feelings;

I feel better about it now. I know the next-door neighbours more now, so not scared ... Now I'm already fine because I'm already four.

Marta, 4-year-old

Learnings and reflections

The key limitation of our implementation of the Program was the limited time scheduled to spend with the residents. The one hour a week allocated may not have been sufficient for some of the children to develop close relationships with the residents. This was compounded by school holidays as well as quarantining children and the class during periods of contagious sickness, and meant that there were times where the Program ceased for up to a month. The importance of being flexible with visit times was essential due to unforeseen events such as meetings, staff and child sickness, funerals and resident events.

Death was a difficult topic to navigate as there is limited literature that tackles how to address death in the early childhood educational setting.

Feedback from colleagues during the pilot program pointed out the need to make sure not to infantilise the residents. In organising the Program, therefore, we made sure that the residents had opportunities to give feedback about the Program.

Wheelchair access to classrooms was an issue for the residents during reciprocal visits as the classrooms were not wheelchair accessible.

The teacher's role is both front and centre in rolling out an effective program. The teacher is central for communicating with all stakeholders; children, residents, colleagues, MP coordinators and families. Inevitably, we found that teachers who had been a part of the Program for a consistent and longer period had deeper relationships with residents and residential staff. Residents were more open in their communication and shared more of their personal life with those teachers.

It is important that several teachers at the same centre are involved with the Program to ensure its sustainability long-term. Teachers will inevitably come and go, and robust engagement from numerous teachers will allow the Program to carry on despite staff turnover. Shared responsibility among the community members is important for the Program as it requires organisation, clear communication and flexibility in itinerary. Hamilton et al. (1999) also highlight the need for designation of staff responsibility in intergenerational programs as many intergenerational programs last less than two years.

Summary

This chapter showcases how young children can develop empathy for others by being involved in community partnership programs. While the intergenerational program was initially developed to foster connections between the children, the elderly and adults of varying abilities, the Program resonates far beyond just the relationships between the children and the residents. The Program has developed a space for learning social etiquette skills, the personal interests and narratives of our neighbours, as well as historical and cultural knowledge. Shared art and musical events have brought the broader communities together, while games, gardening and recreational activities have been a space for companionship in a safe and enjoyable environment. The passing of a resident provided an opportunity for learning about death and the experience of bereavement, while also practising rituals of compassion. Evaluations and feedback from families as well as children's reflective drawings from the intergenerational program has shown the impact the Program has had on teaching children about life and its journey.

Take home messages

- Shared experiences have benefits for all despite the great age divide.
- There is joy in giving and learning.
- Taboo topics can be considered sensitively.
- Community programs promote opportunities for hands-on social and emotional learning.
- Intergenerational programs challenge ageism.
- Guiding literature is important for developing a strong program.
- Elders in our community have a wealth of knowledge and experiences to share with children.

References

Boström, A. K. (2003). *Lifelong learning, intergenerational learning, and social capital: From theory to practice.* Stockholm: Institute of International Education, Stockholm University.

Cartmel, J., Radford, K., Dawson, C., Fitzgerald, A., & Vecchio, N. (2018). Developing an evidenced based intergenerational pedagogy in Australia. *Journal of Intergenerational Relationships*, *16*(1/2), 64–85. doi:10.1080/15350770.2018.1404412

Deans, J., & Wright, S. (2018). *Dance-play and drawing-telling as semiotic tools for young children's learning*. s.l.: Routledge.

Department of Education and Early Childhood Development (DEECD). (2009). *Victorian Early Years Learning and Development Framework*. Melbourne: Early Childhood Strategy Division, Department of Early Childhood Development and Victorian Curriculum Authority.

Department of Education, Employment and Workplace Relations for the Council of Australian Governments (DEEWR). (2009). *Belonging, Being and Becoming: The Early Years Learning Framework for Australia*. Canberra: Australian Government.

Eisner, E. W. (2002). *The arts and the creation of mind*. New Haven: Yale University Press.

Femia, E. E., Zarit, S. H., Blair, C., Jarrott, S. E., & Bruno, K. (2008). Intergenerational pre-school experiences and the young child: Potential benefits to development. *Early Childhood Research Quarterly*, *23*(2), 272–287.

Galbraith, B., Larkin, H., Moorhouse, A., & Oomen, T. (2015). Intergenerational programs for persons with dementia: A scoping review. *Journal of Gerontological Social Work*, *58*(4), 357–378. doi:10.1080/01634372.2015.1008166

Gallagher, C., & Fitzpatrick, A. (2018). "It's a win-win situation" – Intergenerational learning in pre-school and elder care settings: An Irish perspective. *Journal of Intergenerational Relationships*, *16*(1/2), 26–44. doi:10.1080/15350770.2018.1404403

Gigliotti, C., Morris, M., Smock, S., Jarrott, S., & Graham, B. (2005). An intergenerational summer program involving persons with dementia and pre-school children. *Educational Gerontology*, *31*(6), 425–441. doi:10.1080/03601270590928161

Gosine, J., Hawksley, D., & LeMessurier Quinn, S. (2017). Community building through inclusive music making. *Voices: A World Forum for Music Therapy*, *17*, 1.

Hamilton, G., Brown, S., Alonzo, T., Glover, M., Mersereau, Y., & Wilson, P. (1999). Building community for the long term: An intergenerational commitment. *The Gerontologist*, *39*(2), 235–238. doi:10.1093/geront/39.2.235

Heyman, J. C., Gutheil, I. A., & White-Ryan, L. (2011). Pre-school children's attitudes toward older adults: Comparison of intergenerational and traditional day care. *Journal of Intergenerational Relationships*, *9*(4), 435–444. doi:10.1080/15350770.2011.618381

Kellehear, A. (2014). Death education as a public health issue. In J. Stillion & T. Attig (Eds.), *Death, dying and bereavement: Contemporary perspectives and practices* (pp. 221–232). NY: Springer.

Kennedy, C. J., Keeffe, M., Gardner, F., & Farrelly, C. (2017). Making death, compassion and partnership "part of life" in school communities. *Pastoral Care in Education*, *35*(2), 111–123.

Kuehne, V. S., & Melville, J. (2014). The state of our art: A review of theories used in intergenerational program research (2003–2014) and ways forward. *Journal of Intergenerational Relationships*, *12*(4), 317–346. doi:10.1080/15350770.2014.958969

Low, L-F., Russell, F., McDonald, T., & Kauffman, A. (2015). Grandfriends, an intergenerational program for nursing-home residents and pre-schoolers: A randomized trial. *Journal of Intergenerational Relationships*, *13*(3), 227–240. doi:10.1080/15350770.2015.1067130

Minichiello, C., & Jamieson, M. (2006). Ageing. In P. Beilharz & T. Hogan (Eds.), *Sociology; place time and division* (pp. 395–398). Melbourne: Oxford University Press.

Pettigrew, T. F. (2016). In pursuit of three theories: Authoritarianism, relative deprivation, and intergroup contact. *Annu Rev Psychol*, *67*, 1–21. doi:10.1146/annurev-psych-122414-033327

Pettigrew, T. F., & Tropp, L. R. (2006). A meta-analytic test of intergroup contact theory. *J Pers Soc Psychol*, *90*(5), 751–783. doi:10.1037/0022-3514.90.5.751

Steele, M. (2016). How can music build community? Insight from theories and practice of community music therapy. In *Collected Work: Voices: A world forum for music therapy. XVI/2 (2015): Special issue on how music can change your life and the world*. Bergen: GAMUT: Griegakademiets senter for musikkterapiforsking. (AN: 2016-04318) 16 (2).

Chapter 10

Putting it together

Developing well-being in the early years

'Boredom could be a good feeling if you were lying on your bed looking through the window you could feel ok and not bored at all.'

~ Eric, 4-year-old

Overview

This volume is firmly contextualised in the Positive Psychology and Positive Education literature. Whilst Positive Psychology can be considered as an umbrella term which encompasses a range of helpful constructs it focuses on well-being and the building of resilience through the development of a range of skills, such as coping, that have applications for parents, teachers and children. Positive Psychology focuses on aspects of development that are not cognitive alone but addresses aspects that relate to Social Emotional Learning. These aspects of education have become increasingly more relevant in schooling for the future with curriculum requirements being articulated in many educational jurisdictions. This volume offers insights into research and practice in early childhood that builds resilience and well-being through the development of coping skills and more generally through social and emotional learning. It does this in a range of ways that enhances the contribution of teachers and parents.

Putting it together: well-being, development and neuroscience

Constructs such as well-being and resilience are achieved through a strengths-based approach that includes a mindset where the learner sees that growth is possible, and grit and perseverance exist; where there is hope and optimism along with values that include empathy for others and gratitude for one's situation and circumstance. All are part of the learning environment.

Social learning or modelling by parents and teachers is a most powerful educational tool. For example, adults can indicate appreciation of the environment, nature, objects or what people do and children generally follow the adult examples. Children can be encouraged to develop a gratitude journal so as to record or draw things that they have been appreciative of during the day. Gratitude contributes to positive health and well-being and reduces frustration, anger and anxiety.

Whilst there is an interplay between person's and their environments, to the point where both contribute according to development and experiences, nevertheless, the child is an active learner and explorer. There need to be opportunities for satisfying children's curiosity through a range of activities. Whilst no single theory of development provides all the answers, be it Piaget (1952), Vygotsky (1962) or Bronfenbrenner (1979), the interplay between the learner and the environment dominates. The importance of language and its impact on thinking is a concept emphasised by Lev Vygotsky. It again comes into the fore when we operationalise coping, as it is the ability to describe coping, that is, the thoughts, feelings and actions that enables the constructs to be brought into cognitive awareness, to be taught and subsequently to be adopted into a coping repertoire.

Neuroscience is the scientific study of the brain with biologists studying brain anatomy and physiology; Cognitive psychology is the scientific study of the mind with behavioural scientists studying patterns of behaviour and mental processes; whilst education is the study of the learner and educator to focus on learning outcomes. Numerous chapters in this volume focus on the application of research insights to curriculum and educational practice more widely.

The brain, as a major organ of development, continues to mature through adolescence and into adulthood. It is a major organ of executive functioning and regulator of emotions, be it primary (fear, anger, sadness, joy, surprise, disgust) or secondary (shame, embarrassment, guilt, envy and pride). Both positive and negative experiences contribute to learning. What is clear is that learning makes a difference and when it comes to education, given that one size does not fit all children, Raban (2014) points out that we should focus on the *how* of education rather than the *when*.

Social Emotional Learning (SEL)

In the context of education, social and emotional learning has entered the curriculum in many educational communities. The foremost exponents in the English language world are in the US (CASEL) and the UK (SEAL). As these aspects of education have proliferated the curriculum and are expressed in diverse ways there are overriding uniformities that focus on self-awareness, self-management, social awareness and social management.

The important distinction needs to be drawn between Social Emotional Learning as expressed in the various national curricula and social emotional competence as expressed through the skills that are acquired by young people.

Convincing evidence for the benefits of SEL was provided by Durlak, Weissberg, Dymnicki, Taylor and Schellinger (2011) in that instruction has to be sequenced, active, focused and explicit which is what we have done in both the parenting program and the COPE-Resilience program (see Chapters 7 and 9).

Whilst early childhood social emotional programs have proliferated it is interesting to note that none have been found not to be effective in some way. The focus on SEL alone can achieve positive outcomes. A framework program like KidsMatter Early Childhood (2012) focuses on developing emotional literacy, providing resources and supports for educational leaders and teachers and building capacity in the wider community for mental health prevention and support.

General early childhood SEL programs focus on understanding and managing emotions and developing empathy. The use of visual tools, role-plays, games, music and drawing play a part in the programs of instruction, whether scripted or integrated into early childhood classroom practice. Numerous programs are reported from the USA, the UK, Australia and Romania with variations in implementation and programming, but overall there are tangible benefits for children and teachers. As outlined in the Australian curriculum (Belonging, Being and Becoming, EYLF, 2009) the important generic skills relate to having a strong sense of identity, being connected and contributing to the world, having a strong sense of well-being, being confident and involved learners and being effective communicators.

There are many ways to develop social emotional skills that include both scripted and unscripted programs that relate to curriculum demands. All facets of activity can be utilised to teach social emotional skills including music, dance, drama and art. Additionally there are conversations that can be had with children using prompts such as visual tools. Things that concern young children in a particular context can be visually represented, as can the range of possible coping strategies that children may use. These can be helpful or unhelpful and subsequent conversations with children can discuss the benefits or shortcomings of particular ways of coping.

Coping tools

The Early Years Coping Cards (Frydenberg & Deans, 2011) have been developed to enable teachers, parents and children to engage in conversations relating to coping. Beyond these conversation starters and teaching tools it can be helpful to develop empirically derived measurement tools.

In Chapter 5 we describe the adult measures of coping and the early childhood ones. The argument is made that it is important for adults to first understand the concepts of coping and their own coping in order to facilitate the development of their children's coping strategies. When developing the coping tools, we have tried to maintain the language of adult and child coping as closely as is deemed appropriate given the age differential and the fact that adults need to cope with different situations than children. Nevertheless, the broad categorisation of helpful and unhelpful coping assists in achieving common understandings and facilitates the teaching and modelling of coping skills.

Whilst it is possible to measure adult and child coping through empirically developed tools there is a caution against using measurement tools to categorise and label children according to the coping skills that they utilise. We know, for example, that parents and teachers do not assess the same child's coping in exactly the same way, and children themselves respond differently in different situations. It is more helpful to think of how to encourage individuals' critical evaluation of their own coping, be they adults or children. The question could be asked, how would you do it differently next time? What resources and strategies would you use?

Nevertheless, empirically derived measurement tools have their place. None more important than that they help us to see the correlates of coping. We know that there is a two-way interaction between positive coping and well-being. Children who are more likely to use a problem-solving approach are likely to enjoy a more adaptive developmental behavioural trajectory. The implication is that by teaching coping skills you can empower children and help them to increase their well-being.

Anxiety

Anxiety is one of the preeminent concerns in early childhood, with estimates ranging between 10–20% of children being considered to be anxious. Whether it is fear of the dark, fear of being abandoned by a parent or fear of trying something new, there is a clear-cut relationship between anxiety and more emotion-related non-productive coping strategy use. Social anxiety is one of the categories where children are using Negative Coping Emotional Inhibition. Additionally, there is strong evidence (Whalen, Sylvester & Luby, 2017) that behavioural inhibition, which is a temperament style that is characterised by negative emotional response to novel stimuli such as strangers or trying something new, is a powerful known risk factor for developing an anxiety disorder throughout the lifespan. Since relationships continue to be an important source of strength and support throughout the life-time it is recommended that there be a clear focus on teaching good relationship skills and overt expression of concerns from the earliest years of pre-school.

Patterns of anxiety do exist in families, highlighting the importance of modelling and social learning. Additionally, there is clear evidence affirming what might be inferred intuitively, that both adults and children are inclined to use problem-focused coping when a situation is controllable and emotion-focused approaches when situations are perceived as less controllable. Given that it is the emotion-focused strategies that one has to reduce it is important to raise awareness of their usage so they are utilised in an acceptable way.

When a situation is controllable it is more likely to be managed through the use of productive coping strategies rather than non-productive ones, at least for adults and adolescents. However, controllability is not always clear-cut in the early childhood population. For example, in Chapter 6 of the study reported by Yeo, Frydenberg, Northam & Deans (2014) the point is made that for young children controllability is not always clear-cut as, according to parental reporting, children were more likely to use unhelpful strategies when having to eat something they didn't like, rather than having to say goodbye to their parents. As with adults, some situations invoke mixed feelings and it is not always clear how every child will respond. Hence the generalisation problem which makes it important to consider individual children in individual situations rather than being guided by what is reported as normative behaviour.

Throughout the volume we have emphasised the importance of how adult coping impacts how children cope. In Chapter 7 we expanded on these ideas in a parent coping program that incorporates a broad range of core parenting skills that brings children into the conversation. Firstly, there is an emphasis on parent well-being and self-care which is a prerequisite for good parenting. And when it comes to coping, parents are encouraged to seek social support when they need it and not to blame themselves when things go wrong. Secondly, there is a focus on good communication skills whether they be parent–parent or parent–child. These core communication skills include reflective listening, assertiveness and problem-solving. It is important for parents to recognise that it is they who are in charge rather than the children, whatever age they be. Additionally, perhaps the most universally helpful coping strategy is that of problem-solving as in reality each of life's challenges is a problem to be solved.

The program, as is this volume, is underscored by Positive Psychology or what in the context of parenting can be considered to be positive parenting. So, strategies such as noticing a child's strengths in a range of spheres, gratitude and appreciation for what is good and mindfulness as a helpful family practice are encouraged. There are variations to the program. For example, as a self-help mode it can be useful but more importantly when parents participate in a group setting they comment on how much they learn from each other. When it comes to parenting, and for that matter coping, there is always more to be learned. Another variation of the parenting program presented in Chapter 7 is the adaptation for a culturally and linguistically diverse community of parents. The concepts are offered in small groups, sometimes with an interpreter. Additionally, the concepts are reduced to succinct tip sheets which can be readily incorporated into everyday practice in any population. After all we only carry simple messages and reminders around in our minds. Tip sheets are helpful and can be accompanied by visual reminders which may prove to be a more helpful prompt for some rather than words alone.

The final two chapters have a more detailed 'in practice' approach where teaching practices are described. Chapter 8 describes the implementation of the COPE-Resilience program as an exemplar of a classroom-based, teacher-led program that responds to the social emotional aspects of the curriculum and which incorporates 'threads of thinking' and 'big ideas' that now form part of the early learning educational environment. The multimodal learning that is visual, oral, aural, written or kinaesthetic produces growth in both the teacher and the student.

Chapter 9 is a teacher's personal description of an intergenerational program that has evolved as part of the SEL curriculum and piloted by the author. Whilst the program itself is not scripted it is described in sufficient detail to enable a teacher to incorporate the experiences into their early childhood educational practice. The chapter describes activities that are well known in the sector that include drawing-telling, music and singing, games and gardening. What is particular to the intergenerational program is the opportunity afforded to the elderly participants to reminisce about their childhoods such as being a milkman, which captured the children's interest. The merit of such a program is in the main that it is not able to be scripted. The example is provided of a song that proved to be the favourite of one of the residents who was having a birthday. The children wrote out the lyrics which they accompanied with illustrations and presented it to the resident on her birthday. Her reaction was to break out into song. When children sang a song for the resident's birthday the children were asked to clap the number of times that reflected the count of the birthday and on that occasion it meant as many as 93 claps – somewhat challenging for 4-year old children.

As the often taboo topics of aging and death were confronted when an elderly resident passed away, it provided an opportunity for a key learning to be addressed in a safe real-world context. Several times throughout the year when the children performed dances and songs in a choir for the parents and the ELC community, the residents were invited and were emotional at the opportunity to attend the concert and the event provided an opportunity for children's parents to meet the participants.

The children's verbatim responses, such as their quotations included in the front of many of the chapters, clearly highlights the many prosocial reactions that were readily described as part of the program of instruction. Similarly, the children's drawings reflect healthy emotional learning outcomes. The children demonstrated that they could empathise with others and express their emotions in a range of ways.

Several studies have evaluated the COPE-Resilience program with clear beneficial outcomes for students (Cornell et al., 2017; Pang, Frydenberg, Liang & Deans, 2018). In one study where an experienced teacher was compared to the program facilitator the results indicated that children undertaking COPE-R with an experienced teacher facilitator demonstrated the greatest improvement in teacher-rated empathy, prosocial behaviours, coping styles, inhibitory control and problem behaviours (Wu, Alexander, Frydenberg & Deans, 2019). Whilst the findings themselves were not surprising, it does demonstrate that experience matters when teachers are implementing SEL programs that are new and unlikely to be part of their previous teaching repertoire.

In this volume we have introduced theory and a range of applications and practices. The scope of what is possible in the early years is limitless when it comes to providing opportunity for parents and teachers and children to grow their social emotional skills. In a world where there are changing roles and expectations placed on educators to prepare children for the world that awaits them, what remains a constant is the human condition, the need for relational skills, the need for personal support and good parenting practices. The value of Positive Psychology in general and coping skills in particular as contributors to well-being is significant.

References

Bronfenbrenner, U. (1979). Contexts of child rearing: Problems and prospects. *American Psychologist*, 34, 844–850.

Cornell, C., Kiernan, N., Kaufman, D., Dobeee, P., Frydenberg, E., & Deans, J. (2017). Developing social emotional competence in the early years. In E. Frydenberg, A. J. Martin, & R. J. Collie (Eds.) *Social and emotional learning in Australia and the Asia-Pacific* (pp. 391–441). Singapore: Springer.

DEEWR, EYLF. (2009). *Belonging, Being & Becoming: The Early Years Learning Framework for Australia* (pp. c2009). Canberra: Dept. of Education, Employment and Workplace Relations for the Council of Australian Governments.

Durlak, J. A., Weissberg, R. P., Dymnicki, A. B., Taylor, R. D., & Schellinger, K. B. (2011). The impact of enhancing students' social and emotional learning: A meta-analysis of school-based universal interventions. *Child Development*, 82(1), 405–432. doi:10.1111/j.1467-8624.2010.01564.x

Frydenberg, E., & Deans, J. (2011). *The Early Years Coping Cards*. Melbourne, Vic.: ACER Press.

KidsMatter Australia. (2012). KidsMatter Early Childhood introduction. Retrieved 15 May 2016 from www.youtube.com/watch?v=HgyS-SV0Xyg

Pang, D., Frydenberg, E., Liang, R., & Deans, J. (2018). Improving coping skills & promoting social and emotional competence in pre-schoolers : A 5-week COPE-R program. *Journal of Early Childhood Education Research*, 7(2), 1–31.

Piaget, J. (1952). *The origins of intelligence in children*. New York, NY: W.W. Norton & Co.

Raban, B. (2014). Brain research and early childhood education: Directions that could lead us astray. *Australian Educational Leader*, 36(4), 50.

Vygotsky, L. S. (1962). *Thought and language*. Cambridge, MA: MIT Press.

Whalen, D. J., Sylvester, C. M., & Luby, J. L. (2017). Depression and anxiety in pre-schoolers: A review of the past 7 years. *Child and Adolescent Psychiatric Clinics of North America*, 26, 503–522. doi:10.1016/j.chc.2017.02.006

Wu, M. Y., Alexander, M. A., Frydenberg, E., & Deans, J. (2019). Teacher experience matters: Social emotional learning in the early years. *Australian Educational Researchers*.

Yeo, K., Frydenberg, E., Northam, E., & Deans, J. (2014). Coping with stress among pre-school children and associations with anxiety level and controllability of situations. *Australian Journal of Psychology*, 66(2), 93–101. doi:10.1111/ajpy.12047

Index

Page locators in *italics* refer to illustrations, page locators in **bold** refer to tables.

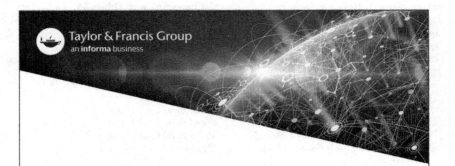

Taylor & Francis Group
an **informa** business

Taylor & Francis eBooks

www.taylorfrancis.com

A single destination for eBooks from Taylor & Francis
with increased functionality and an improved user
experience to meet the needs of our customers.

90,000+ eBooks of award-winning academic content in
Humanities, Social Science, Science, Technology, Engineering,
and Medical written by a global network of editors and authors.

TAYLOR & FRANCIS EBOOKS OFFERS:

A streamlined
experience for
our library
customers

A single point
of discovery
for all of our
eBook content

Improved
search and
discovery of
content at both
book and
chapter level

REQUEST A FREE TRIAL
support@taylorfrancis.com

 Routledge
Taylor & Francis Group

 CRC Press
Taylor & Francis Group